The Crucial Tu Key Campaigns of World War I

The Crucial Turning Points: Key Campaigns of World War I

By

H. Warfield

Vij Books

New Delhi (India)

Published by

Vij Books
(Publishers, Distributors & Importers)
4836/24, 3rd Floor, Ansari Road
Delhi – 110 002
Phone: 91-11-43596460
Mobile: 98110 94883
e-mail: contact@vijpublishing.com
www.vijbooks.in

ISBN: 978-81-19438-23-5 (PB)

Contents

5. Clash of Titans: The Battle of Jutland

The Battle of the Marne: Halting the German Advance

Introduction:

The Battle of the Marne, fought from September 6 to September 12, 1914, was a pivotal moment in the early stages of World War I. It marked the culmination of the German advance into France and the subsequent Allied counterattack that halted the German offensive and ultimately set the stage for the prolonged trench warfare that characterized the Western Front for much of the war.

The battle took place along the Marne River, northeast of Paris, and involved hundreds of thousands of troops from both sides. It was a complex and fluid engagement, characterized by fierce fighting, strategic maneuvering, and high casualties on both sides.

At the outset of World War I, the German army implemented the Schlieffen Plan, a bold strategy aimed at quickly defeating France in the west before turning its attention to Russia in the east. The plan called for a massive right-wing sweep through Belgium and northern France, with the ultimate goal of encircling and capturing Paris.

The German advance into France was swift and initially successful, causing panic and confusion among the Allied forces. However, as the German armies approached the Marne River, they began to encounter stiff resistance from the French and British forces, who were determined to defend Paris at all costs.

The Battle of the Marne was a desperate and decisive struggle. The French commander, General Joseph Joffre, orchestrated a series of counterattacks that surprised and pushed back the German forces. The British Expeditionary Force, under the command of Sir John French, also played a crucial role in the Allied victory, launching attacks that helped to stabilize the front.

The battle ended in a strategic stalemate, with neither side able to achieve a decisive victory. However, the German advance had been effectively halted, and the Allies had succeeded in preventing the capture of Paris. The Battle of the Marne marked a turning point in the war, demonstrating that the conflict would be long and costly, and that neither side would achieve a quick or easy victory.

In this book, we will explore the events leading up to the Battle of the Marne, the course of the battle itself, and its far-reaching consequences. We will examine the strategies and tactics employed by both sides, the experiences of the soldiers who fought in the battle, and the legacy of this momentous engagement in shaping the course of World War I.

The Prelude to Conflict:

The outbreak of World War I in 1914 was the result of a complex web of political, military, and diplomatic factors that had been building for decades. In the years leading up to the war, Europe was divided into two main alliance systems: the Triple Entente, consisting of France, Russia, and Great Britain, and the Triple Alliance, consisting of Germany, Austria-Hungary, and Italy (which later switched sides).

Tensions between these alliances, fueled by nationalism, imperialism, and militarism, were escalating, and a spark was all that was needed to ignite a global conflagration.

The spark came on June 28, 1914, when Archduke Franz Ferdinand, heir to the Austro-Hungarian throne, was assassinated in Sarajevo by a Bosnian Serb nationalist. This event set off a chain reaction of events that led to the outbreak of war. Austria-Hungary, backed by Germany, issued an ultimatum to Serbia, demanding harsh concessions in response to the assassination. When Serbia refused to comply with all of the demands, Austria-Hungary declared war on Serbia on July 28, 1914.

The declaration of war triggered a series of alliances and treaties that drew other European powers into the conflict. Russia, bound by treaty to Serbia, mobilized its army in support of its Slavic ally. Germany, fearing a two-front war with Russia and France, declared war on Russia on August 1 and on France two days later. Germany's invasion of Belgium, a neutral country, to outflank the French army, prompted Great Britain to declare war on Germany on August 4, 1914.

The German strategy, known as the Schlieffen Plan, called for a rapid invasion of France through Belgium, followed by a swift move to the east to confront the Russian army. The plan was based on the assumption that Russia would be slow to mobilize its forces and that France could be quickly defeated, allowing Germany to focus its efforts on the Eastern Front.

The initial phase of the Schlieffen Plan was largely successful, with German forces advancing rapidly through Belgium and northern France. By early September 1914, the

German army was within 30 miles of Paris, and it seemed that a quick victory was within reach.

However, the German advance had stretched its supply lines and exhausted its troops. The French, under the command of General Joseph Joffre, seized the opportunity to launch a counterattack. Joffre reorganized his forces and launched a series of coordinated attacks against the German flanks, forcing them to retreat.

The Battle of the Marne, fought from September 6 to September 12, 1914, was the climax of this counteroffensive. The French and British forces, with the support of newly arrived troops from Paris, succeeded in halting the German advance and pushing them back.

The Battle of the Marne was a costly and bloody conflict, with hundreds of thousands of casualties on both sides. However, it was a strategic victory for the Allies, as it prevented the Germans from achieving a quick victory and forced them to retreat to the Aisne River, where they dug in and established the beginnings of the trench lines that would characterize the Western Front for the next four years.

The Battle of the Marne marked the end of the mobile phase of the war on the Western Front and the beginning of a long and brutal stalemate. It also shattered the illusion of a short, decisive war and demonstrated the destructive power of modern industrial warfare. The events leading up to the Battle of the Marne and the battle itself laid the groundwork for the prolonged and bloody conflict that would come to be known as the Great War.

Contextualizing the European Situation in 1914:

The year 1914 dawned on Europe with an air of tension and uncertainty. The continent had been in a state of relative peace since the end of the Franco-Prussian War in 1871, but underlying this peace were deep-rooted political, economic, and military rivalries that threatened to erupt into conflict.

At the heart of these rivalries were the alliances that had been formed among the major European powers. The Triple Entente, consisting of France, Russia, and Great Britain, was seen as a counterbalance to the Triple Alliance of Germany, Austria-Hungary, and Italy. These alliances were intended to deter aggression and maintain a balance of power, but they also created a complex web of obligations and commitments that could easily draw the continent into war.

The assassination of Archduke Franz Ferdinand, heir to the Austro-Hungarian throne, in Sarajevo on June 28, 1914, was the spark that ignited these tensions. Austria-Hungary, eager to assert its authority in the Balkans, blamed Serbia for the assassination and issued an ultimatum that demanded harsh concessions. Serbia, backed by Russia, refused to comply with all of the demands, and Austria-Hungary declared war on Serbia on July 28, 1914.

The declaration of war set off a chain reaction of alliances and treaties that quickly drew other European powers into the conflict. Russia, bound by treaty to Serbia, mobilized its forces in support of its Slavic ally. Germany, fearing a two-front war with Russia and France, declared war on Russia on August 1 and on France two days later. Germany's invasion of Belgium, a neutral country, to outflank the French army, prompted Great Britain to declare war on Germany on August 4, 1914.

The European situation in 1914 was further complicated by the rise of nationalism and imperialism. Many European nations had overseas empires, and competition for colonies and resources had led to numerous conflicts and tensions.

The assassination of Franz Ferdinand and the subsequent declaration of war highlighted the fragility of the European balance of power and the ease with which a local conflict could escalate into a continent-wide war.

The events of 1914 would set the stage for four years of brutal warfare that would engulf the continent and much of the world. The Great War, as it would come to be known, would change the course of history and have far-reaching consequences that would shape the rest of the 20th century.

The Schlieffen Plan: Germany's Strategy for War on Two Fronts

In the years leading up to World War I, Germany found itself in a precarious military position. It was surrounded by potentially hostile neighbors, with France to the west and Russia to the east. The German General Staff, led by Count Alfred von Schlieffen, devised a bold and ambitious plan to address this strategic dilemma: the Schlieffen Plan.

The Schlieffen Plan was a strategic military plan designed to allow Germany to quickly defeat France in the west before turning its full attention to Russia in the east. The plan was based on several key assumptions and strategic calculations.

First, the plan assumed that Russia would be slow to mobilize its forces due to its vast size and infrastructure limitations. Germany believed that it could quickly defeat France within six weeks, before turning its armies eastward to face the Russian threat.

Second, the plan called for a massive right-wing sweep through neutral Belgium and northern France, bypassing the heavily fortified French-German border region known as the Alsace-Lorraine. This maneuver was intended to outflank the French army and quickly encircle and capture Paris, the French capital.

Third, the plan relied heavily on the use of railways to rapidly mobilize and deploy German forces. The German General Staff calculated the exact timing and routes for the movement of troops, supplies, and equipment to ensure maximum efficiency and speed.

The execution of the Schlieffen Plan began on August 4, 1914, with the German invasion of Belgium. German forces quickly advanced through Belgium and into northern France, meeting stiff resistance from Belgian, French, and British forces along the way.

However, the Schlieffen Plan ultimately failed to achieve its objectives. The rapid advance of German forces slowed as they encountered supply shortages, logistical difficulties, and increasing French resistance. The Battle of the Marne, fought from September 6 to September 12, 1914, marked the turning point of the plan, as French and British forces launched a successful counterattack that forced the Germans to retreat.

While the Schlieffen Plan failed to achieve its goal of a quick victory over France, it had far-reaching consequences for the course of World War I. The failure of the plan led to the establishment of the Western Front, a system of entrenched defensive positions that stretched from the North Sea to the Swiss border. This stalemate would persist for much of the war, resulting in years of bloody trench warfare and countless casualties on both sides.

Mobilization and Initial Military Movements:

In the summer of 1914, as tensions in Europe reached a boiling point, the Great Powers began mobilizing their armed forces in preparation for war. Mobilization was a complex and time-consuming process that involved calling up reserves, assembling troops, and deploying them to the front lines. Mobilization plans had been developed years in advance and were based on various scenarios and contingencies.

Germany, as the instigator of the conflict, was the first to mobilize. On July 31, 1914, Germany issued an ultimatum to Russia demanding that it demobilize its forces. When Russia refused, Germany declared war on Russia on August 1 and began mobilizing its army. The German mobilization plan, known as the Schlieffen Plan, called for a rapid invasion of France through neutral Belgium, followed by a swift move to the east to confront the Russian army.

France, bound by treaty to Russia, began mobilizing its forces in support of its ally. The French mobilization plan focused on quickly deploying troops to the eastern frontier to defend against a possible German invasion. The French also launched a series of offensive operations in Alsace-Lorraine to divert German forces from the main thrust of the German attack.

Russia, with the largest army in Europe, mobilized its forces more slowly than expected due to logistical challenges and the vastness of its territory. However, by mid-August, Russian forces were advancing into East Prussia, prompting Germany to shift troops from the western front to the eastern front to counter the Russian threat.

In response to the German invasion of Belgium, Great Britain, which had a treaty obligation to protect Belgian neutrality, declared war on Germany on August 4, 1914. British mobilization focused on assembling and deploying its expeditionary force to the Western Front, where it would play a crucial role in halting the German advance.

The mobilization and initial military movements of August 1914 set the stage for the opening phase of World War I. The rapid mobilization of millions of soldiers and the massive logistical effort required to support them demonstrated the scale and scope of the conflict that was about to unfold. The decisions made during this critical period would shape the course of the war and have far-reaching consequences for Europe and the world.

The German Advance:

In the summer of 1914, the German army launched a massive military offensive as part of the Schlieffen Plan, aimed at quickly defeating France in the west before turning its attention to Russia in the east. The German advance was swift and initially successful, catching the Allies off guard and causing panic and confusion among their ranks.

The German army, well-trained and well-equipped, made rapid progress through Belgium and northern France, relying on the speed and flexibility of its troops to outmaneuver and outflank the French and British forces. The use of railways to quickly move troops and supplies to the front lines gave the Germans a significant advantage in terms of mobility and logistics.

As the German army advanced, it encountered stiff resistance from Belgian, French, and British forces determined to defend their territory. Battles were fought along the way as the Germans sought to secure key objectives and strategic positions. Despite heavy fighting and mounting casualties, the German army continued to advance, pushing deeper into French territory.

By early September 1914, the German army was within striking distance of Paris, and it seemed that a quick victory was within reach. However, the rapid advance had stretched the German supply lines and exhausted its troops. The French, under the command of General Joseph Joffre, seized the opportunity to launch a counterattack.

The Battle of the Marne, fought from September 6 to September 12, 1914, marked the climax of the German advance. The French and British forces, with the support of newly arrived troops from Paris, succeeded in halting the German advance and pushing them back. The battle ended in a strategic stalemate, with neither side able to achieve a decisive victory.

The failure of the German advance to achieve its objectives had far-reaching consequences for the rest of the war. It marked the end of the mobile phase of the war on the Western Front and the beginning of a long and brutal stalemate. The events of 1914 demonstrated the destructive power of modern industrial warfare and set the stage for four years of bloody conflict that would reshape the map of Europe and the world.

The German Invasion of Belgium and France:

On August 4, 1914, Germany launched its invasion of Belgium, marking the beginning of its offensive on the Western Front during World War I. The invasion was a critical component of the Schlieffen Plan, the German strategy aimed at quickly defeating France and then turning east to face Russia. The invasion of Belgium was necessary to outflank the heavily fortified Franco-German border and quickly advance into France.

The invasion of Belgium was met with immediate international condemnation, as Belgium had been a neutral country since the Treaty of London in 1839. The violation of Belgian neutrality prompted Great Britain, which had a treaty obligation to protect Belgian neutrality, to declare war on Germany on the same day.

The German invasion of Belgium was characterized by a series of atrocities committed against the civilian population. German troops engaged in widespread looting, pillaging, and destruction of property, and there were numerous reports of civilians being killed or mistreated. These actions fueled international outrage and galvanized support for the Allied cause.

As German forces advanced through Belgium, they encountered stiff resistance from Belgian, French, and British forces. The Belgian army, though outnumbered and outgunned, fought bravely to defend their country. The Battle of Liège, fought from August 5 to August 16, 1914, was the first major engagement of the invasion and resulted in a German victory, but at a higher cost than anticipated.

The German advance into France through Belgium was initially successful, with German troops making rapid progress towards Paris. However, logistical challenges, supply shortages, and increasing resistance from Allied forces slowed the German advance. The Battle of the Marne, fought from September 6 to September 12, 1914, marked the turning point of the invasion, as French and British forces launched a successful counterattack that forced the Germans to retreat.

The German invasion of Belgium and France had far-reaching consequences for the rest of the war. It led to a long and bloody stalemate on the Western Front, where both sides dug in and established entrenched defensive positions. The atrocities committed during the invasion also had a profound impact on public opinion and the conduct of the war, contributing to the escalation of hostilities and the total war mentality that characterized World War I.

The German Invasion: Initial Successes and Rapid Progress Towards Paris

In August 1914, the German army launched a massive invasion of Belgium and France as part of the Schlieffen Plan, a bold strategy aimed at quickly defeating France in the west before turning its full attention to Russia in the east. The invasion began on August 4, 1914, with the German army crossing into Belgium, violating its neutrality, and advancing towards France.

The German invasion met with immediate success, as the German army quickly overran Belgian defenses and pushed deep into Belgian territory. The speed and ferocity of the German advance caught the Allies off guard, and Belgian resistance, though valiant, was ultimately unable to halt the German onslaught.

As German forces advanced through Belgium, they encountered stiff resistance from Belgian, French, and British forces. However, the German army, well-trained and well-equipped, was able to outmaneuver and outflank the Allied forces, using its superior mobility and firepower to great effect.

One of the key objectives of the German invasion was the capture of Paris, the French capital. The German plan called for a rapid advance through Belgium and northern France, bypassing the heavily fortified Franco-German border region known as the Alsace-Lorraine, and encircling and capturing Paris from the northwest.

By early September 1914, the German army was within striking distance of Paris, and it seemed that a quick victory was within reach. The French government, fearing the fall of the capital, was evacuated to Bordeaux, and there was widespread panic and confusion among the civilian population.

However, the rapid advance of the German army had stretched its supply lines and exhausted its troops. The French, under the command of General Joseph Joffre, seized the opportunity to launch a counterattack.

The Battle of the Marne, fought from September 6 to September 12, 1914, marked the climax of the German advance. The French and British forces, with the support of newly arrived troops from Paris, succeeded in halting the German advance and pushing them back. The battle ended in a strategic stalemate, with neither side able to achieve a decisive victory.

The initial successes of the German invasion and the rapid progress towards Paris demonstrated the effectiveness of the German military strategy and the superiority of its army. However, the failure to capture Paris and achieve a quick victory had far-reaching consequences for the rest of the war, setting the stage for a long and bloody stalemate on the Western Front.

Challenges and Obstacles Faced by the Allied Forces:

During the early stages of World War I, the Allied forces faced a number of significant challenges and obstacles as they sought to counter the German advance on the Western Front. These challenges were both strategic and logistical in nature, and they tested the resolve and ingenuity of Allied commanders and troops.

1.   Numerical Inferiority: One of the key challenges faced by the Allies was their numerical inferiority compared

to the German forces. The German army was well-trained, well-equipped, and highly motivated, and it enjoyed a significant numerical advantage in the early stages of the war. This meant that the Allies often found themselves outnumbered and outgunned on the battlefield.

2.   Logistical Challenges: The rapid mobilization and deployment of troops and supplies posed significant logistical challenges for the Allies. The sheer scale of the conflict meant that vast quantities of food, ammunition, and equipment had to be transported to the front lines, often over long distances and under difficult conditions. The poor state of the roads and railways in many parts of Europe further complicated the logistical effort.

3.   Communication and Coordination: The Allied forces were made up of troops from a number of different countries, each with its own command structure, language, and culture. This made communication and coordination between Allied forces difficult, and it sometimes led to misunderstandings and conflicting orders.

4.   Defensive Disadvantages: The Allies were largely on the defensive in the early stages of the war, as they sought to halt the German advance. This meant that they often had to fight from entrenched positions, which made them vulnerable to artillery fire and made it difficult to launch effective counterattacks.

5.   Supply Shortages: The rapid pace of the German advance meant that the Allies often struggled to keep their troops supplied with food, ammunition, and equipment. This was particularly true during the Battle of the Marne, when the French and British forces were stretched to their limits and had to rely on hastily improvised supply lines.

6.   Despite these challenges, the Allied forces were able to halt the German advance and ultimately turn the tide of the war in their favor. The Battle of the Marne, in particular, demonstrated the resilience and determination of the Allied forces in the face of overwhelming odds, and it marked a turning point in the early stages of World War I.

The French Response in the Battle:

In the early stages of World War I, the French army faced a formidable challenge as it sought to counter the German advance on the Western Front. The French response to the German invasion was characterized by a combination of strategic flexibility, tactical innovation, and sheer determination.

1.   Strategic Reorganization: In response to the German invasion, the French commander-in-chief, General Joseph Joffre, reorganized his forces and adopted a flexible defense strategy. Joffre recognized the importance of the initiative and sought to regain it through aggressive counterattacks and rapid redeployments of his forces.

2.   Counterattacks and Offensive Operations: One of the key elements of the French response was a series of counterattacks and offensive operations aimed at disrupting the German advance and regaining lost territory. These operations were often costly and were not always successful, but they succeeded in keeping the German forces off balance and preventing them from achieving a decisive breakthrough.

3.   Defense of Paris: The French response also focused on the defense of Paris, the French capital, which was threatened by the German advance. Joffre ordered the creation of a new army, the Sixth Army, to defend the city,

and he also called upon the civilian population to help with the construction of fortifications and the digging of trenches.

4.   Coordination with Allied Forces: The French response was closely coordinated with the actions of the British Expeditionary Force (BEF) and other Allied forces. Despite differences in language, culture, and command structures, the Allies were able to work together effectively to halt the German advance.

5.   Morale and Spirit: Perhaps the most important aspect of the French response was the morale and spirit of the French troops. Despite heavy casualties and the hardships of war, the French soldiers fought bravely and tenaciously, determined to defend their country and repel the invader.

The French response to the German invasion was ultimately successful, as the French and Allied forces were able to halt the German advance at the Battle of the Marne in September 1914. The battle marked a turning point in the war and demonstrated the resilience and determination of the French army in the face of overwhelming odds.

Joffre's Reorganization of the French Army:

General Joseph Joffre, the French commander-in-chief during the early stages of World War I, played a crucial role in reorganizing and revitalizing the French army in response to the German invasion of France in 1914. Joffre's reorganization efforts were instrumental in the French army's ability to halt the German advance and ultimately turn the tide of the war in favor of the Allies.

1.   Strategic Flexibility: One of Joffre's key innovations was his emphasis on strategic flexibility. Recognizing the fluid and dynamic nature of modern warfare, Joffre sought to create an army that was capable of rapid movement and

quick redeployment to meet changing battlefield conditions. He emphasized the importance of maintaining the initiative and taking advantage of opportunities as they arose.

2.   Centralized Command: Joffre centralized command and control of the French army, streamlining the chain of command and reducing bureaucratic inefficiencies. This allowed for more rapid decision-making and greater coordination of military operations.

3.   Creation of New Armies: In response to the German invasion, Joffre created several new armies, including the Sixth Army, which was tasked with defending Paris. These new armies were composed of fresh troops and were intended to bolster the French defenses and provide additional firepower and manpower.

4.   Tactical Innovation: Joffre introduced several tactical innovations, including the use of artillery barrages to soften enemy defenses before infantry attacks and the use of airplanes for reconnaissance and artillery spotting. These innovations helped to improve the effectiveness of French military operations and gave the French army a crucial edge on the battlefield.

5.   Morale and Discipline: Joffre placed a strong emphasis on morale and discipline within the French army. He worked to instill a sense of pride and esprit de corps among the troops, emphasizing the importance of their role in defending France and repelling the German invader.

Joffre's reorganization of the French army was a critical factor in the French army's ability to withstand the German onslaught in 1914. His strategic vision, tactical innovations, and emphasis on morale and discipline helped to create a more agile, responsive, and effective fighting force that was able to halt the German advance and ultimately emerge victorious in the Battle of the Marne.

The Strategic Decision to Counterattack:

One of the most crucial strategic decisions made by the Allied forces during the early stages of World War I was the decision to launch a counterattack against the advancing German army. This decision, led by French commander-in-chief General Joseph Joffre, was a bold and risky move that ultimately played a key role in halting the German advance and turning the tide of the war in favor of the Allies.

1.   Recognition of the Threat: The decision to counterattack was based on a recognition of the threat posed by the advancing German army. The German forces had made rapid progress through Belgium and northern France and were within striking distance of Paris. The Allied commanders understood the importance of stopping the German advance before it could achieve a decisive breakthrough.

2.   Seizing the Initiative: By launching a counterattack, the Allied forces sought to seize the initiative and regain control of the battlefield. The German army had been on the offensive, dictating the course of the war, and the Allies recognized the need to take decisive action to change the momentum of the conflict.

3.   Exploiting Weaknesses: The counterattack was also based on an assessment of weaknesses in the German position. The rapid German advance had stretched their supply lines and exhausted their troops, making them vulnerable to a determined Allied assault. The counterattack aimed to exploit these weaknesses and throw the German army off balance.

4.   Strategic Flexibility: The decision to counterattack demonstrated the strategic flexibility of the Allied commanders. Rather than adhering rigidly to a defensive posture, they were willing to take risks and launch offensive operations when the situation demanded it. This flexibility would prove crucial in the fluid and dynamic nature of modern warfare.

5.   Coordination and Cooperation: The success of the counterattack depended on close coordination and cooperation between the Allied forces. Despite differences in language, culture, and command structures, the Allies were able to work together effectively to plan and execute the counterattack, demonstrating the strength of the Allied coalition.

The decision to counterattack was not without risks, and the Battle of the Marne, fought from September 6 to September 12, 1914, was a costly and bloody engagement. However, it was ultimately successful, as the French and British forces, with the support of newly arrived troops from Paris, succeeded in halting the German advance and pushing them back. The Battle of the Marne marked a turning point in the war and demonstrated the resolve and determination of the Allied forces in the face of overwhelming odds.

The Role of French Leadership and Morale:

During the early stages of World War I, French leadership played a crucial role in rallying the French army and civilian population in the face of the German invasion. Led by General Joseph Joffre, the French military leadership exhibited resilience, adaptability, and strategic acumen, which were instrumental in turning the tide of the war in favor of the Allies.

1.   Joffre's Strategic Vision: General Joffre, the French commander-in-chief, demonstrated a clear strategic vision in his response to the German invasion. He reorganized the French army, adopted a flexible defense strategy, and launched a series of counterattacks aimed at disrupting the German advance. Joffre's leadership was characterized by decisiveness and a willingness to take risks, which were crucial in the fluid and dynamic nature of modern warfare.

2.   Morale and Esprit de Corps: French leadership played a key role in maintaining the morale and esprit de corps of the French army. Despite heavy casualties and the hardships of war, French soldiers remained determined and resolute, motivated by a sense of duty and patriotism instilled by their leaders. French commanders led by example, often placing themselves at the forefront of the fighting, which inspired their troops to follow suit.

3.   Civilian Leadership: French civilian leaders also played an important role in maintaining morale and unity on the home front. The French government, under Prime Minister René Viviani, worked closely with military leaders to coordinate the war effort and mobilize the civilian population. Propaganda and public speeches emphasized the importance of the war effort and the need for sacrifice to defend France.

4.   National Unity: French leadership was instrumental in fostering a sense of national unity and solidarity among the French people. Despite political differences and regional divisions, the French population rallied behind the government and the military in a united effort to repel the German invader. This sense of unity was crucial in sustaining the French war effort during the difficult early years of the war.

5.   Legacy and Impact: The role of French leadership and morale in World War I had a lasting impact on French society and military doctrine. The experience of the war, and the leadership demonstrated by figures such as Joffre, helped to shape the French military's approach to warfare and its understanding of national defense. French leadership and morale were crucial factors in the Allied victory in World War I, and they continue to be celebrated as examples of resilience and determination in the face of adversity.

The Battle Unfolds:

The campaign of the Battle of the Marne unfolded over several days in September 1914 and was a pivotal moment in World War I. The battle marked the end of the German advance into France and the beginning of a long and bloody stalemate on the Western Front. The unfolding of the battle can be divided into several key phases:

1.   Initial German Advance: The battle began with the German army's rapid advance through Belgium and northern France, as part of the Schlieffen Plan. The German forces made significant progress and were within striking distance of Paris by early September 1914.

2.   French Counterattack: The turning point of the battle came with the French counterattack, led by General Joseph Joffre. Joffre reorganized his forces and launched a series of coordinated attacks against the German flanks, forcing them to retreat.

3.   British Involvement: The British Expeditionary Force (BEF), under the command of Sir John French, played a crucial role in the battle. The BEF's timely arrival and aggressive actions helped to bolster the French defense and contributed to the success of the counterattack.

4.   Trench Warfare: The Battle of the Marne marked the beginning of trench warfare on the Western Front. Both sides dug in and established entrenched defensive positions, leading to a prolonged and bloody stalemate that would characterize the rest of the war.

5.   Human Cost: The Battle of the Marne was a costly and bloody conflict, with hundreds of thousands of casualties on both sides. The battle demonstrated the destructive power of modern industrial warfare and foreshadowed the horrors to come in the years ahead.

6.   Strategic Implications: The outcome of the Battle of the Marne had far-reaching strategic implications. It prevented the Germans from achieving a quick victory in the west and forced them to retreat to the Aisne River, where they dug in and established the beginnings of the trench lines that would characterize the Western Front for the next four years.

Overall, the Battle of the Marne was a pivotal moment in World War I and demonstrated the importance of leadership, strategy, and determination in the face of adversity. The battle set the stage for the long and brutal conflict that would follow and had a profound impact on the course of the war.

Initial Clashes and Skirmishes along the Marne River:

The Battle of the Marne, fought from September 6 to September 12, 1914, was preceded by a series of initial clashes and skirmishes along the Marne River as the German and Allied forces maneuvered and jockeyed for position. These early engagements set the stage for the larger battle that would unfold in the days to come.

1.   German Advance Stalls: As the German army approached the Marne River, they encountered stiffening

resistance from the retreating French forces. The rapid pace of the German advance had stretched their supply lines and exhausted their troops, making them vulnerable to a determined Allied defense.

2.   French Rear Guard Actions: The French army, under the command of General Joseph Joffre, conducted a series of rear guard actions along the Marne River, slowing the German advance and buying time for the French and British forces to prepare their defenses.

3.   British Expeditionary Force Engages: The British Expeditionary Force (BEF), under the command of Sir John French, also played a role in these early skirmishes. The BEF conducted a series of delaying actions, engaging the advancing German forces and inflicting casualties while withdrawing in an orderly fashion.

4.   Artillery Duels and Reconnaissance: In addition to infantry skirmishes, there were also several artillery duels and reconnaissance missions along the Marne River. Both sides used artillery to shell enemy positions and disrupt their movements, while reconnaissance aircraft were used to gather information about enemy troop movements and positions.

5.   Fluid and Dynamic Situation: The situation along the Marne River was fluid and dynamic, with both sides constantly maneuvering and probing for weaknesses. The early clashes and skirmishes were a prelude to the larger battle that would unfold in the days to come, as both sides prepared to engage in a decisive showdown.

The initial clashes and skirmishes along the Marne River were a precursor to the larger battle that would follow. They demonstrated the determination and resilience of the French and Allied forces and set the stage for the eventual Allied victory in the Battle of the Marne.

Tactical Maneuvers and Engagements on the Battlefield:

The Battle of the Marne was characterized by a series of tactical maneuvers and engagements as the German and Allied forces sought to gain the upper hand on the battlefield. These maneuvers were marked by fluidity and dynamism, with both sides constantly adapting to changing circumstances and seeking to exploit weaknesses in the enemy's position.

1. Flanking Maneuvers: One of the key tactics employed by both sides was flanking maneuvers, where troops would attempt to outflank and encircle the enemy. The Germans, in particular, sought to execute a wide-ranging envelopment of the Allied forces, while the Allies attempted to turn the German flanks and disrupt their advance.

2. Artillery Barrages: Artillery played a crucial role in the battle, with both sides using artillery barrages to soften enemy defenses before infantry attacks. The Germans, in particular, made extensive use of artillery, employing heavy bombardments to break through Allied lines and create openings for their infantry.

3. Infantry Assaults: Infantry assaults were a common feature of the battle, with troops on both sides engaging in close-quarters combat as they sought to capture enemy positions. These assaults were often brutal and costly, with high casualties on both sides.

4. Counterattacks and Defensive Actions: Both the Germans and the Allies launched counterattacks and defensive actions throughout the battle as they sought to maintain or regain control of key positions. These actions

were often decisive in determining the outcome of individual engagements.

5.   Use of Reserves: Both sides also made use of reserves to reinforce their front lines and exploit opportunities as they arose. The timely arrival of reserves could often turn the tide of a battle and secure victory for the side that employed them.

6.   Terrain and Weather: The terrain and weather also played a role in shaping the tactical maneuvers and engagements on the battlefield. The Marne River, with its wooded banks and marshy terrain, presented obstacles to both sides, while the hot weather and dust kicked up by marching troops made conditions challenging for soldiers on both sides.

Overall, the tactical maneuvers and engagements on the battlefield during the Battle of the Marne were marked by fluidity, intensity, and a constant struggle for advantage. The battle demonstrated the importance of tactical skill, adaptability, and resilience in modern warfare, and it set the stage for the long and bloody conflict that would follow on the Western Front.

The Ebb and Flow of the Fighting:

The Battle of the Marne was a dynamic and fluid conflict, characterized by a series of advances and retreats as both sides sought to gain the upper hand. The ebb and flow of the fighting were influenced by a variety of factors, including strategic decisions, tactical maneuvers, and the resilience of the troops.

1.   Initial German Advance: The battle began with a rapid advance by the German army, which pushed deep into French territory and threatened Paris. The German forces

made significant gains in the early days of the battle, putting the Allies on the defensive.

2.   Allied Counterattack: The turning point of the battle came with the Allied counterattack, led by General Joseph Joffre. The French and British forces launched a series of coordinated attacks against the German flanks, forcing them to retreat.

3.   German Retreat: The German retreat was initially orderly, as they sought to regroup and establish new defensive positions along the Aisne River. However, the retreat soon became more chaotic as the German forces came under increasing pressure from the advancing Allies.

4.   Stalemate: The battle eventually settled into a stalemate, with both sides digging in and establishing entrenched defensive positions. The Allied forces were unable to break through the German lines, and the Germans were unable to dislodge the Allies from their positions.

5.   Tactical Maneuvers: Throughout the battle, both sides engaged in a series of tactical maneuvers, including flanking attacks, artillery barrages, and infantry assaults. These maneuvers were often costly and brutal, with high casualties on both sides.

6.   Impact of Reserves: The timely arrival of reserves played a crucial role in the ebb and flow of the fighting. The arrival of fresh troops could often turn the tide of a battle and secure victory for the side that employed them.

7.   Terrain and Weather: The terrain and weather also played a role in shaping the ebb and flow of the fighting. The Marne River, with its wooded banks and marshy terrain, presented obstacles to both sides, while the hot weather

and dust kicked up by marching troops made conditions challenging for soldiers on both sides.

Overall, the ebb and flow of the fighting during the Battle of the Marne were a testament to the resilience and determination of the troops on both sides. The battle demonstrated the brutal and unforgiving nature of modern industrial warfare and set the stage for the long and bloody conflict that would follow on the Western Front.

Crisis and Decision:

The Battle of the Marne reached a critical juncture as both the German and Allied forces faced significant challenges and had to make crucial decisions that would shape the outcome of the battle and the course of the war.

1. German Supply Shortages: As the German army advanced into France, its supply lines became stretched and overextended. The rapid pace of the advance had outstripped the ability of the supply system to keep up, leading to shortages of food, ammunition, and other essential supplies. This logistical crisis hampered the German army's ability to sustain its offensive and maintain its momentum.

2. Allied Defensive Stance: The Allied forces, under the command of General Joseph Joffre, adopted a defensive stance along the Marne River, seeking to hold the line and prevent a further German advance. The decision to go on the defensive was a calculated one, aimed at conserving strength and waiting for an opportunity to launch a counterattack.

3. German Strategic Reassessment: Faced with supply shortages and stiffening Allied resistance, the German high command was forced to reassess its strategic objectives. The initial plan had been to quickly defeat France and then turn east to face Russia, but the realities of the battlefield forced a

change in plans. The German army was ordered to dig in and establish defensive positions along the Aisne River, marking the end of the rapid advance into France.

4.   Allied Counterattack: The Allied forces seized the initiative and launched a series of counterattacks against the retreating German army. The French and British forces, supported by newly arrived troops from Paris, pushed the Germans back and inflicted heavy casualties.

5.   Strategic Stalemate: The Battle of the Marne ended in a strategic stalemate, with neither side able to achieve a decisive victory. The German army had been halted and forced to retreat, but the Allies were unable to deliver a knockout blow and dislodge the Germans from their entrenched positions.

6.   Impact on the War: The Battle of the Marne had far-reaching consequences for the rest of the war. It marked the end of the mobile phase of the war on the Western Front and the beginning of a long and bloody stalemate. The battle also demonstrated the importance of logistics, supply lines, and decision-making at the highest levels of command in modern warfare.

Critical Moments in the Battle:

The Battle of the Marne, fought from September 6 to September 12, 1914, was a complex and dynamic conflict with several critical moments that shaped its outcome and the course of World War I.

1.   The German Advance Towards Paris: In the early days of the battle, the German army made rapid progress towards Paris, coming within striking distance of the French capital. The fall of Paris would have been a devastating blow

to the Allied cause and could have potentially led to a quick German victory in the west.

2.   The French Decision to Counterattack: The turning point of the battle came with the French decision to launch a counterattack against the retreating German army. Led by General Joseph Joffre, the French and British forces launched a series of coordinated attacks that forced the Germans to retreat and halted their advance towards Paris.

3.   The British Expeditionary Force's Stand at the Marne: The British Expeditionary Force (BEF), under the command of Sir John French, played a crucial role in the battle. The BEF's stand along the Marne River helped to stabilize the Allied line and prevent a further German advance.

4.   The Battle for the Ourcq River: One of the decisive engagements of the Battle of the Marne was the Battle for the Ourcq River. The French Sixth Army, under General Michel Maunoury, launched a successful attack against the German First Army, forcing them to retreat and helping to secure the Allied victory.

5.   The German Retreat and Entrenchment: Faced with stiffening Allied resistance and supply shortages, the German army was forced to retreat and establish defensive positions along the Aisne River. This marked the end of the rapid German advance into France and the beginning of a long and bloody stalemate on the Western Front.

6.   The Strategic Stalemate: The Battle of the Marne ended in a strategic stalemate, with neither side able to achieve a decisive victory. The battle demonstrated the resilience and determination of the Allied forces and set the stage for the long and brutal conflict that would follow on the Western Front.

Overall, the Battle of the Marne was a critical moment in World War I and demonstrated the importance of leadership, strategy, and tactical acumen in modern warfare. The battle marked a turning point in the war and had far-reaching consequences for the rest of the conflict.

Command Decisions and Strategic Gambles:

The Battle of the Marne was marked by a series of command decisions and strategic gambles that had far-reaching consequences for the outcome of the battle and the course of World War I.

1.   Joffre's Decision to Counterattack: Perhaps the most significant command decision of the battle was General Joseph Joffre's decision to launch a counterattack against the retreating German army. Joffre recognized the importance of seizing the initiative and regaining control of the battlefield, and his decision to go on the offensive ultimately proved decisive in halting the German advance.

2.   French Strategic Flexibility: Throughout the battle, Joffre demonstrated a willingness to adapt his strategy to changing circumstances. He reorganized his forces, launched counterattacks, and made use of reserves in order to keep the Germans off balance and exploit weaknesses in their position.

3.   German High Command's Strategic Mistakes: On the German side, the high command made several strategic mistakes that contributed to their defeat. The decision to split their forces and send troops east to face the Russians weakened their position in France and left them vulnerable to the Allied counterattack.

4.   British Expeditionary Force's Stand: The decision of the British Expeditionary Force (BEF) to stand and

fight along the Marne River was another critical command decision. Despite being outnumbered and outgunned, the BEF's determined defense helped to stabilize the Allied line and prevent a further German advance.

5. Strategic Gambles: Both sides took strategic gambles during the battle, with varying degrees of success. The German army's initial plan to quickly defeat France and then turn east to face Russia was a bold gamble that nearly succeeded but ultimately failed. The Allied decision to launch a counterattack was also a gamble, but one that paid off and helped to turn the tide of the battle in their favor.

6. Legacy and Impact: The command decisions and strategic gambles made during the Battle of the Marne had a lasting impact on the course of World War I. The battle demonstrated the importance of leadership, strategy, and tactical acumen in modern warfare and set the stage for the long and bloody conflict that would follow on the Western Front.

The Turning Point: The Decision to Halt the German Advance

The Battle of the Marne was a critical turning point in World War I, marked by the decision of the Allied forces, under the command of General Joseph Joffre, to halt the German advance into France. This decision, made in early September 1914, had far-reaching consequences for the outcome of the battle and the course of the war.

1. Recognition of the Threat: The decision to halt the German advance was based on a recognition of the threat posed by the advancing German army. The rapid pace of the German advance had caught the Allies off guard, and there was a real danger that the Germans could achieve a decisive breakthrough and capture Paris.

2.   Strategic Reassessment: The decision to halt the German advance represented a strategic reassessment by the Allied high command. Rather than continue to retreat and seek a more defensible position further south, Joffre decided to take a stand along the Marne River and launch a counterattack against the retreating German army.

3.   Seizing the Initiative: By halting the German advance and launching a counterattack, Joffre sought to seize the initiative and regain control of the battlefield. The decision was a bold one, as it involved taking the offensive against a numerically superior enemy, but it ultimately proved to be decisive in turning the tide of the battle.

4.   Logistical Challenges: Halted the German advance was not without its challenges. The rapid pace of the German advance had stretched their supply lines and exhausted their troops, making them vulnerable to a determined Allied assault. The decision to halt the advance and dig in along the Marne River gave the Allies time to rest and resupply their troops, while the Germans struggled to maintain their momentum.

5.   Tactical Maneuvers: The decision to halt the German advance and launch a counterattack involved a series of tactical maneuvers, including flanking attacks, artillery barrages, and infantry assaults. These maneuvers were often costly and brutal, but they ultimately succeeded in pushing the Germans back and securing victory for the Allies.

The decision to halt the German advance at the Battle of the Marne was a critical moment in World War I and demonstrated the importance of leadership, strategy, and tactical acumen in modern warfare. The battle marked a turning point in the war and had far-reaching consequences for the rest of the conflict.

The Aftermath of the Battle of the Marne:

The Battle of the Marne, fought from September 6 to September 12, 1914, was a pivotal moment in World War I and had far-reaching consequences for the course of the war and the future of Europe. The aftermath of the battle was marked by a number of significant developments that would shape the rest of the conflict.

1.   Strategic Stalemate: The Battle of the Marne ended in a strategic stalemate, with neither side able to achieve a decisive victory. The German army, which had been forced to retreat, dug in and established defensive positions along the Aisne River, marking the beginning of a long and bloody stalemate on the Western Front.

2.   End of the Schlieffen Plan: The Battle of the Marne spelled the end of the German Schlieffen Plan, which had aimed to quickly defeat France and then turn east to face Russia. The failure of the plan to achieve its objectives meant that the war on the Western Front would become a protracted and bloody struggle of attrition.

3.   Trench Warfare: The aftermath of the Battle of the Marne saw the establishment of entrenched defensive positions along the Western Front. Both sides dug in and fortified their positions, leading to a stalemate that would last for the next four years. Trench warfare became the dominant form of warfare on the Western Front, characterized by static, defensive positions and brutal, costly attacks.

4.   Human Cost: The Battle of the Marne was a costly battle, with hundreds of thousands of casualties on both sides. The aftermath of the battle saw the French and German armies exhausted and depleted, with both sides facing the grim reality of a long and brutal war of attrition.

5.   Impact on Civilians: The Battle of the Marne had a profound impact on the civilian population of France and Belgium. The battle was fought on French soil, and the civilian population was caught in the crossfire, with many towns and villages destroyed and thousands of civilians killed or displaced.

6.   Political Consequences: The aftermath of the Battle of the Marne had significant political consequences. In France, the victory at the Marne was celebrated as a triumph of French resilience and determination, and it helped to bolster national unity and morale. In Germany, the failure of the Schlieffen Plan led to criticism of the military leadership and contributed to a sense of disillusionment with the war.

7.   Impact on the War: The Battle of the Marne had far-reaching consequences for the rest of the war. It marked the end of the mobile phase of the war on the Western Front and the beginning of a long and bloody stalemate. The battle also demonstrated the importance of logistics, supply lines, and decision-making at the highest levels of command in modern warfare.

Overall, the Battle of the Marne was a critical moment in World War I and had a profound impact on the course of the conflict. Its aftermath saw the establishment of trench warfare on the Western Front and set the stage for the long and brutal war that would follow.

Assessing the Consequences of the Battle of the Marne:

The Battle of the Marne, fought from September 6 to September 12, 1914, was a pivotal moment in World War I with significant consequences that would shape the course of the conflict and the future of Europe. Assessing the consequences of the battle reveals its profound impact on military strategy, the civilian population, and the broader political and social landscape.

1.   **Military Strategy:**

> The Battle of the Marne marked the end of the Schlieffen Plan, the German strategy to quickly defeat France and then turn east to face Russia. The failure of the plan led to a prolonged stalemate on the Western Front, characterized by trench warfare.

> The battle demonstrated the importance of logistics, supply lines, and decision-making at the highest levels of command in modern warfare. It highlighted the challenges of conducting offensive operations in the face of entrenched defensive positions.

2.   **Civilian Impact:**

> The Battle of the Marne had a profound impact on the civilian population, especially in France and Belgium. Many towns and villages were destroyed, and thousands of civilians were killed or displaced.

> The battle also had economic consequences, as the war disrupted agriculture, industry, and trade, leading to shortages and inflation.

3.   **Political and Social Consequences:**

> In France, the victory at the Marne was celebrated as a triumph of French resilience and determination. It helped to bolster national unity and morale, and it played a key role in shaping French identity and memory of the war.

➢ In Germany, the failure of the Schlieffen Plan led to criticism of the military leadership and contributed to a sense of disillusionment with the war. The battle also had political repercussions, as it led to the establishment of a military dictatorship in Germany.

4.   Impact on the War:

➢ The Battle of the Marne marked the beginning of a long and bloody stalemate on the Western Front. Trench warfare became the dominant form of warfare, characterized by static, defensive positions and brutal, costly attacks.

➢ The battle also had strategic implications for the rest of the war. It prevented the Germans from achieving a quick victory in the west and forced them to retreat to the Aisne River, where they dug in and established the beginnings of the trench lines that would characterize the Western Front for the next four years.

5.   Legacy:

➢ The Battle of the Marne left a lasting legacy on military strategy and tactics. It demonstrated the importance of preparedness, flexibility, and adaptability in modern warfare, and it influenced military thinking for years to come.

➢ The battle also had a profound impact on the civilian population and the broader political and social landscape of Europe. It contributed to the shaping of national identities and the memory of the war, and it played a key role in shaping the post-war world order.

Strategic Implications for Both Sides:

The Battle of the Marne had profound strategic implications for both the Allied and German forces, shaping the course of World War I and influencing military strategy for years to come.

1.   Allied Forces:

> For the Allies, the Battle of the Marne was a crucial victory that halted the German advance and prevented the fall of Paris. The victory boosted Allied morale and demonstrated that the German army was not invincible.

> The battle marked the beginning of a long and bloody stalemate on the Western Front, with both sides digging in and establishing entrenched defensive positions. This stalemate would characterize the rest of the war and lead to a war of attrition.

2.   German Forces:

> For the Germans, the Battle of the Marne was a strategic setback that ended their hopes for a quick victory in the west. The failure of the Schlieffen Plan forced the Germans to retreat and establish defensive positions along the Aisne River.

> The battle also had a psychological impact on the German army and the civilian population, as it shattered the myth of German invincibility and raised doubts about the ultimate outcome of the war.

3.   Trench Warfare:

➤ The Battle of the Marne marked the beginning of trench warfare on the Western Front. Both sides dug in and fortified their positions, leading to a stalemate that would last for the next four years. Trench warfare was characterized by static, defensive positions and brutal, costly attacks.

4. Impact on the War:

➤ The Battle of the Marne had far-reaching consequences for the rest of the war. It prevented the Germans from achieving a quick victory in the west and forced them to focus on a war of attrition.

➤ The battle also demonstrated the importance of logistics, supply lines, and decision-making at the highest levels of command in modern warfare. It highlighted the challenges of conducting offensive operations in the face of entrenched defensive positions.

5. Legacy:

➤ The Battle of the Marne left a lasting legacy on military strategy and tactics. It demonstrated the importance of preparedness, flexibility, and adaptability in modern warfare, and it influenced military thinking for years to come.

➤ The battle also had a profound impact on the civilian population and the broader political and social landscape of Europe. It contributed to the shaping of national identities and the memory of the war, and it played a key role in shaping the post-war world order.

Legacy and Significance of the Battle of the Marne in World War I:

The Battle of the Marne, fought from September 6 to September 12, 1914, had a profound legacy and significance in World War I, shaping the course of the conflict and influencing military strategy and tactics for years to come.

1.   End of German Offensive: The Battle of the Marne marked the end of the German offensive on the Western Front and the failure of the Schlieffen Plan. The German army, which had been on the verge of a decisive victory, was forced to retreat and establish defensive positions along the Aisne River.

2.   Establishment of Trench Warfare: The Battle of the Marne marked the beginning of trench warfare on the Western Front. Both sides dug in and fortified their positions, leading to a stalemate that would last for the next four years. Trench warfare was characterized by static, defensive positions and brutal, costly attacks.

3.   Psychological Impact: The Battle of the Marne had a profound psychological impact on both sides. For the Allies, it was a crucial victory that boosted morale and demonstrated that the German army was not invincible. For the Germans, it shattered the myth of German invincibility and raised doubts about the ultimate outcome of the war.

4.   Influence on Military Strategy: The Battle of the Marne influenced military strategy and tactics for years to come. It demonstrated the importance of preparedness, flexibility, and adaptability in modern warfare, and it highlighted the challenges of conducting offensive operations in the face of entrenched defensive positions.

5.   National Identity and Memory: The Battle of the Marne played a key role in shaping national identities and the memory of the war. In France, it was celebrated as a triumph of French resilience and determination, and it helped to bolster national unity and morale. In Germany, it led to criticism of the military leadership and contributed to a sense of disillusionment with the war.

6.   Long-Term Consequences: The Battle of the Marne had far-reaching consequences for the rest of the war and the post-war world order. It prevented the Germans from achieving a quick victory in the west and forced them to focus on a war of attrition. It also contributed to the shaping of the post-war world order and laid the groundwork for the Treaty of Versailles.

Overall, the Battle of the Marne was a critical moment in World War I and had a profound impact on the course of the conflict. Its legacy and significance would be felt long after the guns fell silent on the Western Front.

Remembering the Marne:

The Battle of the Marne, fought in September 1914, holds a significant place in the collective memory of World War I, particularly in France. Remembering the Marne encompasses both the historical events of the battle and the broader cultural and symbolic meanings it has come to represent.

1.   National Identity and Unity: In France, the Battle of the Marne is remembered as a moment of national unity and resilience. It symbolizes the French people's determination to defend their homeland against German aggression and their refusal to surrender in the face of overwhelming odds.

2.   Military Strategy and Tactics: The Battle of the Marne is also remembered for its impact on military strategy

and tactics. It marked the end of the mobile phase of the war on the Western Front and the beginning of trench warfare. The battle demonstrated the importance of preparedness, flexibility, and adaptability in modern warfare.

3.   Human Cost: Remembering the Battle of the Marne also involves reflecting on the human cost of the conflict. The battle was a bloody and brutal affair, with hundreds of thousands of soldiers killed, wounded, or missing on both sides. It serves as a reminder of the sacrifice and suffering endured by those who fought in World War I.

4.   Cultural and Artistic Representations: The Battle of the Marne has been depicted in various cultural and artistic forms, including literature, art, and film. These representations often focus on the heroism and sacrifice of the soldiers who fought in the battle and the impact it had on the course of the war.

5.   Legacy and Significance: The Battle of the Marne has a lasting legacy and significance that extends beyond its historical context. It is seen as a turning point in World War I, marking the end of the German advance in the west and the beginning of a long and bloody stalemate on the Western Front. It also played a key role in shaping the post-war world order.

6.   International Commemoration: The Battle of the Marne is not only remembered in France but also commemorated internationally. It is a reminder of the importance of remembering and honoring the sacrifices made by those who fought in World War I and the need to learn from the lessons of the past.

In conclusion, remembering the Battle of the Marne is not only about recalling the historical events of the battle but also about reflecting on its broader significance and legacy. It serves as a reminder of the human cost of war, the importance of national unity and resilience, and the enduring impact of historical events on the present day.

Commemoration and Remembrance of the Battle of the Marne:

The Battle of the Marne, fought in September 1914, is commemorated and remembered in various ways, both in France and internationally. The battle holds a significant place in the collective memory of World War I and is seen as a pivotal moment in the conflict. Commemoration and remembrance of the battle serve to honor the sacrifices made by those who fought and died, as well as to reflect on the broader significance of the battle in shaping the course of the war and its impact on the world.

1.   Annual Commemorations: In France, the Battle of the Marne is commemorated annually on September 6th, the anniversary of the start of the battle. Commemorative events are held at various locations associated with the battle, including the Marne River and the city of Paris. These events often include memorial services, wreath-laying ceremonies, and reenactments of key moments from the battle.

2.   Military Parades: Military parades are often held as part of the commemorations, featuring marching bands, military units, and veterans. These parades serve to honor the memory of those who fought in the battle and to pay tribute to their bravery and sacrifice.

3.   Memorials and Monuments: There are several memorials and monuments dedicated to the Battle of the Marne, both in France and in other countries. These memorials serve as a permanent reminder of the battle and its significance, and they provide a place for people to pay their respects and remember the fallen.

4.   Educational Programs: Schools and educational institutions often incorporate the Battle of the Marne into their curriculum as part of their efforts to educate students about World War I and its impact. This helps to ensure that the memory of the battle is passed down to future generations.

5.   Cultural Representations: The Battle of the Marne has been depicted in various forms of art and culture, including literature, art, and film. These cultural representations help to keep the memory of the battle alive and ensure that it remains a part of the collective consciousness.

6.   International Commemoration: The Battle of the Marne is not only commemorated in France but also internationally. Many countries that participated in World War I hold their own commemorations to honor the memory of the battle and its significance in the wider context of the war.

In conclusion, commemoration and remembrance of the Battle of the Marne are important ways of honoring the memory of those who fought and died in the battle, as well as reflecting on its broader significance in shaping the course of World War I and its impact on the world.

Monuments, Memorials, and Commemorations of the Battle of the Marne:

The Battle of the Marne, fought in September 1914, is commemorated and remembered through various monuments, memorials, and commemorations in France and around the world. These sites and events serve to honor the sacrifices made by those who fought and died in the battle and to ensure that the memory of the battle is preserved for future generations.

1.   The Monument of the Marne (Monument de la Marne): Located in Mondement-Montgivroux, France, this monument commemorates the Battle of the Marne. It consists of a large obelisk surrounded by statues representing various aspects of the battle, including soldiers, nurses, and civilians. The monument serves as a focal point for annual commemorations of the battle.

2.   The Memorial of the Marne (Mémorial de la Marne): Located in Dormans, France, this memorial is dedicated to the memory of the soldiers who fought and died in the Battle of the Marne. It features a large ossuary containing the remains of unidentified soldiers, as well as a museum that tells the story of the battle and its significance.

3.   The Monument to the Victory of the Marne (Monument à la Victoire de la Marne): Located in Vitry-le-François, France, this monument commemorates the Allied victory in the Battle of the Marne. It features a large bronze statue of a French soldier standing atop a German eagle, symbolizing the defeat of the German army.

4.   The Marne Cemetery (Cimetière de la Marne): Located near Châlons-en-Champagne, France, this cemetery is the final resting place for many of the soldiers who died in the Battle of the Marne. The cemetery is maintained by the French government and is a solemn reminder of the human cost of the battle.

5.   Annual Commemorations: The Battle of the Marne is commemorated annually on September 6th, the anniversary of the start of the battle. Commemorative events are held at various locations associated with the battle, including the Marne River and the city of Paris. These events often include memorial services, wreath-laying ceremonies, and reenactments of key moments from the battle.

6.   International Commemorations: The Battle of the Marne is not only commemorated in France but also internationally. Many countries that participated in World War I hold their own commemorations to honor the memory of the battle and its significance in the wider context of the war.

Overall, monuments, memorials, and commemorations of the Battle of the Marne play an important role in ensuring that the memory of the battle is preserved and that the sacrifices made by those who fought and died are remembered and honored.

Personal Stories and Accounts from Participants of the Battle of the Marne:

The Battle of the Marne, fought in September 1914, left a lasting impact on those who participated, both soldiers and civilians. Personal stories and accounts from participants provide a poignant and often harrowing glimpse into the realities of war and the human experience during this pivotal moment in history.

1.   Soldiers' Experiences:

➤ Many soldiers who fought in the Battle of the Marne experienced the horrors of trench warfare for the first time. They endured long periods of waiting, often in squalid and dangerous conditions, punctuated by moments of intense combat.

➤ Soldiers faced the constant threat of death or injury from artillery shells, machine gun fire, and gas attacks. They also had to contend with disease, malnutrition, and the harsh realities of life in the trenches.

2. **Civilians' Stories:**

➤ Civilians living in the vicinity of the battle also experienced the impact of war. Many were forced to flee their homes to escape the fighting, while others remained behind and faced the destruction of their towns and villages.

➤ Civilians often had to contend with shortages of food, water, and other essential supplies, as well as the presence of occupying forces. The war brought hardship and suffering to many civilian populations, leaving lasting scars on communities.

3. **Letters and Diaries:**

➤ Letters and diaries written by soldiers and civilians during the Battle of the Marne provide a glimpse into the thoughts, feelings, and experiences of those who lived through the conflict. These personal accounts offer a unique perspective on the human cost of war and the resilience of the human spirit.

➤ Many of these letters and diaries have been preserved and are now housed in archives and museums, providing a valuable resource for historians and researchers studying the battle and its impact.

4. **Legacy and Remembrance:**

➤ The personal stories and accounts of those who participated in the Battle of the Marne serve as a reminder of the human cost of war and the importance of remembering and honoring the sacrifices made by those who fought and died.

➢ These stories also highlight the resilience and courage of those who lived through the battle, and their determination to rebuild their lives and communities in the aftermath of the conflict.

In conclusion, personal stories and accounts from participants of the Battle of the Marne provide a powerful and moving testament to the impact of war on individuals and communities. They offer a glimpse into the lived experience of those who endured the conflict, and they remind us of the importance of remembering and honoring their sacrifices.

Verdun: The Longest Battle

Introduction:

The Battle of Verdun, fought from February to December 1916, stands as one of the most iconic and devastating battles of World War I. Situated in northeastern France, Verdun was a strategic fortress town surrounded by a ring of forts, making it a key point in the French defense system. The German High Command, under the leadership of Chief of Staff Erich von Falkenhayn, identified Verdun as a target for a massive offensive, believing that capturing the town would severely weaken French morale and resolve.

Historical Context:

- ➤ By 1916, World War I had been raging for over a year, with neither side gaining a decisive advantage on the Western Front. The German strategy had shifted to a policy of attrition, aiming to bleed the French army white and force France out of the war.

- ➤ The French, on the other hand, were determined to hold their ground and defend their territory at all costs. Verdun, with its symbolic and strategic importance, became a focal point of this determination.

Strategic Importance:

➤ Verdun was situated on high ground overlooking the Meuse River, giving it a commanding position in the region. The town was also surrounded by a ring of forts, making it a formidable defensive position.

➤ For the Germans, capturing Verdun would not only deal a significant blow to French morale but would also threaten the entire Allied position on the Western Front. It was seen as a key stepping stone to eventual victory.

German Offensive:

➤ The German offensive at Verdun began on February 21, 1916, with a massive artillery barrage that lasted for ten hours. This was followed by a ground assault by three German armies, aiming to capture the town and surrounding forts.

➤ The initial German advances were swift, and they managed to capture several key forts and gain ground. However, the French army, under the command of General Philippe Pétain, mounted a determined defense and refused to yield.

French Defense:

➤ The French defense of Verdun was characterized by a strategy of defense in depth, with reserves held back to counter-attack and regain lost ground. Pétain famously declared, "They shall not pass," symbolizing the French determination to hold the line.

➤ The French army also made effective use of artillery and trench warfare tactics, inflicting heavy casualties on the advancing German forces and slowing their progress.

The Battle of Attrition:

➢ The Battle of Verdun quickly devolved into a battle of attrition, with both sides suffering heavy casualties. The Germans hoped to "bleed France white," but the French resolve and determination to hold Verdun remained unbroken.

➢ The battle dragged on for months, with neither side able to gain a decisive advantage. The town and surrounding area were devastated by artillery fire and trench warfare, leaving a lasting scar on the landscape and the people who lived there.

Legacy and Memory:

➢ The Battle of Verdun has left a lasting legacy on both France and Germany. For the French, it is a symbol of national resilience and determination in the face of overwhelming odds. For the Germans, it is a reminder of the futility and horror of war.

➢ The battlefield at Verdun is now a memorial and a place of remembrance, honoring the thousands of soldiers who lost their lives in the battle. It serves as a poignant reminder of the human cost of war and the importance of peace.

The Battle of Verdun stands as a testament to the brutality and devastation of World War I. It was a battle of attrition that tested the limits of human endurance and resolve. The legacy of Verdun serves as a reminder of the horrors of war and the need to strive for peace and understanding in the world.

The Strategic Importance of Verdun:

Verdun, a small town in northeastern France, held immense strategic importance during World War I due to its location, fortifications, and symbolic value. Situated on high ground overlooking the Meuse River, Verdun was surrounded by a ring of forts that made it a key point in the French defensive system. Its capture would not only threaten the French line but also potentially open the way for a German advance towards Paris and other key French cities.

1.   Strategic Location:

Verdun's location on high ground gave it a commanding position in the region, allowing for observation and control of the surrounding area. It also provided a natural defensive barrier against enemy advances.

The town was situated at a strategic crossroads, with roads and railways converging on it from all directions. This made it a key logistical hub for the French army, facilitating the movement of troops and supplies to the front lines.

2.   Fortifications:

Verdun was surrounded by a ring of forts, including Fort Douaumont and Fort Vaux, which were considered among the strongest in France. These forts were equipped with heavy artillery and provided a formidable defensive position.

The forts were linked by a network of trenches and defensive works, creating a strong defensive line that was difficult for enemy forces to penetrate.

3.   Symbolic Value:

Verdun held great symbolic value for the French people. It was a symbol of French resistance and determination, having been the site of several battles during France's history, including the Franco-Prussian War.

The French government and military viewed Verdun as a symbol of national pride and were determined to defend it at all costs, regardless of the human and material toll.

4.   German Objectives:

The German High Command, under the leadership of Chief of Staff Erich von Falkenhayn, identified Verdun as a key objective in their strategy for 1916. They believed that capturing Verdun would not only deal a significant blow to French morale but also force the French army to commit its reserves, weakening its overall position on the Western Front.

The Germans hoped that a successful offensive at Verdun would lead to a breakthrough on the Western Front and potentially pave the way for a negotiated peace with France.

5.   French Defensive Strategy:

The French were well aware of the strategic importance of Verdun and were determined to defend it at all costs. General Philippe Pétain, who was in charge of the French defense, adopted a strategy of defense in depth, with reserves held back to counter-attack and regain lost ground.

The French also made effective use of artillery and trench warfare tactics, inflicting heavy casualties on the advancing German forces and slowing their progress.

In conclusion, the strategic importance of Verdun during World War I cannot be overstated. Its capture would have had far-reaching consequences for the French army and the

Allied position on the Western Front. The Battle of Verdun, with its immense human and material cost, stands as a testament to the strategic significance of this small town in northeastern France.

Overview of the Location and Significance of the Verdun Fortress:

Verdun, located in northeastern France, has long been a site of strategic importance due to its geographical features and historical significance. The town is situated on a meander of the Meuse River, which forms a natural defensive barrier on three sides, making it an ideal location for a fortress. Verdun's strategic location made it a key stronghold in the region, and its fortifications played a crucial role in the defense of France during various conflicts throughout history.

1.   Geographical Features:

Verdun is located on a series of hills overlooking the Meuse River, providing a commanding view of the surrounding area. The town is surrounded by steep valleys and ravines, making it difficult for enemy forces to approach.

The Meuse River, which flows to the west of Verdun, acted as a natural barrier, further enhancing the town's defensive position. The river's meandering course created a loop around Verdun, creating a narrow neck of land that was easy to defend.

2.   Historical Significance:

Verdun has a long history dating back to Roman times when it was known as "Verodunum." The town has been the site of several battles and sieges throughout history, including during the Franco-Prussian War in 1870-71.

The fortress at Verdun was significantly expanded and modernized in the late 19th and early 20th centuries as part of France's efforts to strengthen its eastern defenses against potential German aggression.

3.   Fortifications:

The Verdun fortress consisted of a ring of forts and defensive works surrounding the town. The forts were equipped with heavy artillery and machine guns, and were designed to withstand prolonged sieges.

The two main forts, Fort Douaumont and Fort Vaux, were among the largest and most heavily fortified in France. They were situated on high ground overlooking the town, providing a commanding view of the surrounding area.

4.   Strategic Importance:

The Verdun fortress was strategically located at the junction of several major roads and railways, making it a key logistical hub for the French army. It also served as a rallying point for French forces in the event of an enemy invasion.

The fortress's proximity to the German border made it a likely target for a German offensive, and its capture would have opened up a direct route to Paris and other key French cities.

In conclusion, the Verdun fortress was a key defensive position in northeastern France, with a long history of strategic importance. Its fortifications played a crucial role in the defense of France during World War I and its location and significance made it a prime target for German forces. The Battle of Verdun, fought in 1916, would become one of the longest and bloodiest battles of World War I, highlighting the fortress's importance in the conflict.

German Objectives and French Determination to Defend Verdun:

The Battle of Verdun, fought from February to December 1916, was a pivotal moment in World War I, characterized by the German objective to capture the strategic fortress town of Verdun and the French determination to defend it at all costs. This clash of objectives and determination would result in one of the longest and most grueling battles of the war, with profound consequences for both sides.

1.   German Objectives:

The German High Command, under Chief of Staff Erich von Falkenhayn, identified Verdun as a key objective in their strategy for 1916. They believed that capturing Verdun would not only deal a significant blow to French morale but also force the French army to commit its reserves, weakening its overall position on the Western Front.

Falkenhayn saw Verdun as a "spearhead" aimed at the heart of France, a symbolic and strategic target that, if captured, could potentially lead to a breakthrough on the Western Front and pave the way for a negotiated peace with France.

The German plan called for a massive artillery bombardment followed by a ground assault by three German armies, aiming to overwhelm the French defenses and capture Verdun before the French could reinforce their positions.

2.   French Determination to Defend Verdun:

Verdun held great symbolic and strategic importance for the French people and military. It was seen as a symbol of French resistance and determination, having been the site of several battles during France's history, including the Franco-Prussian War.

The French government and military were determined to defend Verdun at all costs, regardless of the human and material toll. General Philippe Pétain, who was in charge of the French defense, adopted a strategy of defense in depth, with reserves held back to counter-attack and regain lost ground.

Pétain famously declared, "Ils ne passeront pas" ("They shall not pass"), symbolizing the French determination to hold the line at Verdun and prevent the Germans from achieving their objectives.

3.   The Battle of Verdun:

The German offensive at Verdun began on February 21, 1916, with a massive artillery bombardment that lasted for ten hours. This was followed by a ground assault by three German armies, aiming to capture the town and surrounding forts.

The initial German advances were swift, and they managed to capture several key forts and gain ground. However, the French defense, bolstered by the determination of Pétain and the French soldiers, gradually stiffened, and the Germans were unable to achieve a decisive breakthrough.

The battle quickly devolved into a battle of attrition, with both sides suffering heavy casualties. The French defense held firm, and despite repeated German assaults, Verdun remained in French hands.

4.   Legacy and Impact:

The Battle of Verdun had a profound impact on both sides and on the course of the war. For the Germans, it was a costly failure that drained their resources and manpower and failed to achieve their objectives.

For the French, it was a symbol of their determination and resilience in the face of overwhelming odds. The defense of Verdun became a rallying cry for the French people and served to strengthen their resolve to continue the fight against Germany.

The Battle of Verdun also had a lasting impact on the landscape and people of the region. The town and surrounding area were devastated by artillery fire and trench warfare, leaving a lasting scar on the land and the people who lived there.

In conclusion, the Battle of Verdun was a pivotal moment in World War I, characterized by the clash of German objectives and French determination. The battle, with its immense human and material cost, highlighted the brutal and unforgiving nature of modern warfare and left a lasting impact on both sides.

The Build-Up to the Battle of Verdun:

The Battle of Verdun, fought from February to December 1916, was preceded by a series of events and developments that set the stage for one of the most grueling and significant battles of World War I. The build-up to the battle involved strategic planning, military preparations, and a shifting balance of power on the Western Front.

### 1.	Strategic Planning:

By early 1916, the war on the Western Front had reached a stalemate, with neither side able to gain a decisive advantage. The German High Command, under Chief of Staff Erich von Falkenhayn, sought to break the deadlock through a strategy of attrition.

Falkenhayn identified Verdun, with its strategic location and symbolic value, as a key target for a massive offensive. He believed that capturing Verdun would deal a significant blow to French morale and force the French army to commit its reserves, weakening its overall position on the Western Front.

2. Military Preparations:

The German offensive at Verdun was meticulously planned and carefully executed. It began with a massive artillery bombardment on February 21, 1916, which lasted for ten hours and targeted the French positions and fortifications around Verdun.

Following the artillery barrage, three German armies launched a ground assault, aiming to capture the town and surrounding forts. The initial German advances were swift, and they managed to capture several key forts and gain ground.

3. French Defense:

The French were well aware of the strategic importance of Verdun and were determined to defend it at all costs. General Philippe Pétain, who was in charge of the French defense, adopted a strategy of defense in depth, with reserves held back to counter-attack and regain lost ground.

The French defense was bolstered by the determination of Pétain and the French soldiers, who refused to yield despite the heavy losses and relentless German assaults.

4. Shift in Balance of Power:

The Battle of Verdun marked a shift in the balance of power on the Western Front. Prior to Verdun, the German army had been on the offensive, with the French and British forces primarily on the defensive.

However, the French defense at Verdun, coupled with the British offensive at the Somme later in 1916, signaled a reversal of fortunes for the Allies, eventually leading to their eventual victory on the Western Front.

In conclusion, the build-up to the Battle of Verdun was characterized by strategic planning, military preparations, and a shifting balance of power on the Western Front. The battle would prove to be one of the longest and most grueling of World War I, with profound consequences for both sides.

The Initial German Plans and Preparations for the Offensive at Verdun:

The Battle of Verdun, fought from February to December 1916, was preceded by meticulous planning and careful preparations by the German High Command. The initial German plans and preparations for the offensive at Verdun were aimed at achieving a decisive breakthrough on the Western Front and forcing the French army into a position of surrender or collapse. This involved a comprehensive strategy that encompassed both military and logistical aspects.

1.   Strategic Objectives:

The German High Command, under Chief of Staff Erich von Falkenhayn, identified Verdun as a key target for a major offensive in 1916. Falkenhayn believed that capturing Verdun would not only deal a significant blow to French morale but also force the French army to commit its reserves, weakening its overall position on the Western Front.

Falkenhayn saw Verdun as a symbol of French national pride and believed that its capture would have a demoralizing effect on the French people, potentially leading to a collapse of the French war effort.

2.   Military Planning:

The German offensive at Verdun was part of a broader strategy aimed at breaking the deadlock on the Western Front and achieving a decisive victory over the Allies. The plan called for a massive artillery bombardment followed by a ground assault by three German armies, aiming to capture Verdun and the surrounding forts.

The German plan relied heavily on the element of surprise and the use of overwhelming force to achieve a quick and decisive victory. The initial phase of the offensive was designed to quickly capture key objectives and gain control of the high ground overlooking Verdun.

3.   Logistical Preparations:

The logistical preparations for the offensive at Verdun were extensive and complex. The German army stockpiled vast quantities of artillery shells, ammunition, and supplies in preparation for the offensive, ensuring that they would have the resources needed to sustain a prolonged campaign.

The German army also constructed a network of supply lines and communication trenches to support the advancing troops and ensure that they could be quickly resupplied and reinforced.

4.   Deployment of Forces:

The German offensive at Verdun was launched by the 5th Army, under the command of Crown Prince Wilhelm, and the 3rd Army, under the command of General Fritz von Below. These armies were supported by the 1st and 7th Armies, which were held in reserve.

The German forces were organized into several army corps, each with its own objectives and targets. The overall goal was to capture Verdun and the surrounding forts as quickly as possible and establish a strong defensive position to repel any French counterattacks.

5.   Artillery Preparation:

The artillery preparation for the offensive at Verdun was unprecedented in its scale and intensity. The German army amassed over 1,200 artillery pieces, including heavy siege guns and howitzers, which were used to bombard the French positions and fortifications around Verdun.

The artillery bombardment began on February 21, 1916, and lasted for ten hours, unleashing a barrage of shells that destroyed much of the French defenses and softened up the enemy positions for the ground assault.

6.   Infantry Assault:

Following the artillery bombardment, the German infantry launched a ground assault on the French positions. The initial advances were swift, and the Germans managed to capture several key forts and gain ground. However, the French defense, led by General Philippe Pétain, gradually stiffened, and the Germans were unable to achieve a decisive breakthrough.

In conclusion, the initial German plans and preparations for the offensive at Verdun were comprehensive and carefully coordinated. The German High Command believed that capturing Verdun would be a decisive blow to French morale and would force the French army into a position of surrender or collapse. However, the French defense, bolstered by Pétain and the determination of the French soldiers, proved to be more resilient than expected, leading to a prolonged and bloody battle that would have profound consequences for both sides.

French Defensive Measures and Troop Deployments at Verdun:

The French defense of Verdun, from February to December 1916, was characterized by a combination of strategic planning, tactical flexibility, and sheer determination. The French were well aware of the strategic importance of Verdun and were determined to defend it at all costs. This involved a comprehensive strategy that encompassed both defensive measures and troop deployments.

1.   Strategic Planning:

The French defense of Verdun was led by General Philippe Pétain, who was appointed commander of the Verdun sector in February 1916. Pétain adopted a strategy of defense in depth, with reserves held back to counter-attack and regain lost ground.

Pétain also focused on strengthening the defensive fortifications around Verdun, improving communications and supply lines, and bolstering the morale and discipline of the French troops.

2.   Tactical Flexibility:

The French defense at Verdun was characterized by tactical flexibility and adaptability. French troops were trained to react quickly to changing battlefield conditions and to make use of the terrain to their advantage.

The French also made effective use of artillery and trench warfare tactics, inflicting heavy casualties on the advancing German forces and slowing their progress.

3.   Defensive Fortifications:

The French fortifications around Verdun consisted of a series of forts and defensive works, including Fort Douaumont and Fort Vaux, which were among the largest and most heavily fortified in France. These forts were equipped with heavy artillery and machine guns and provided a formidable defensive position.

The French also constructed a network of trenches, barbed wire entanglements, and defensive works to protect their positions and impede the advance of the German forces.

4.   Troop Deployments:

The French deployed a significant number of troops to defend Verdun, including infantry, artillery, and support units. Troops were rotated in and out of the front lines to prevent exhaustion and maintain morale.

French reserves were held in readiness behind the front lines, ready to be deployed to counter-attack and reinforce the defensive positions as needed.

5.   Supply and Communication:

The French army made efforts to improve supply and communication lines to Verdun, ensuring that troops could be quickly resupplied and reinforced. This involved the construction of new roads and railways, as well as the use of motor vehicles and bicycles to transport supplies and messages.

6.   Morale and Discipline:

Pétain placed a strong emphasis on maintaining the morale and discipline of the French troops at Verdun. He visited the front lines regularly, personally inspecting the troops and boosting their morale with speeches and encouragement.

Pétain also implemented strict discipline measures, cracking down on desertion and cowardice, to ensure that the troops remained focused and determined in the face of the enemy.

In conclusion, the French defense of Verdun was characterized by strategic planning, tactical flexibility, and sheer determination. The French troops, under the leadership of Pétain, fought bravely and tenaciously, repelling repeated German assaults and holding the line at Verdun. Their efforts would ultimately prevent the Germans from achieving their objectives and would have a lasting impact on the course of the war.

The German Offensive Begins:

The Battle of Verdun, one of the most significant and brutal battles of World War I, began on February 21, 1916, with a massive German offensive aimed at capturing the strategic fortress town of Verdun. The German High Command, under the leadership of Chief of Staff Erich von Falkenhayn, had identified Verdun as a key target for a major offensive, believing that its capture would deal a significant blow to French morale and force the French army to commit its reserves, weakening its overall position on the Western Front. The German offensive was meticulously planned and carefully executed, but it would soon encounter fierce resistance from the French defenders, leading to a prolonged and bloody battle that would have profound consequences for both sides.

Artillery Bombardment:

The German offensive at Verdun began with a massive artillery bombardment that lasted for ten hours, unleashing a barrage of shells on the French positions and fortifications around Verdun. The artillery bombardment was intended to soften up the enemy positions and destroy the French defenses, making it easier for the German infantry to advance.

The German artillery barrage was one of the most intense and sustained of the war, with over 1,200 artillery pieces, including heavy siege guns and howitzers, participating in the bombardment. The French positions were subjected to a relentless barrage of high-explosive and shrapnel shells, causing widespread destruction and chaos among the defenders.

Ground Assault:

Following the artillery bombardment, three German armies launched a ground assault on the French positions around Verdun. The initial advances were swift, and the Germans managed to capture several key forts and gain ground. However, the French defense, led by General Philippe Pétain, gradually stiffened, and the Germans were unable to achieve a decisive breakthrough.

The German infantry encountered fierce resistance from the French defenders, who fought bravely and tenaciously to hold their ground. The French troops, many of whom were seasoned veterans of previous battles, were well trained and well equipped, and they made effective use of artillery and trench warfare tactics to repel the German assaults.

Capture of Fort Douaumont:

One of the early successes for the Germans was the capture of Fort Douaumont, one of the largest and most heavily fortified forts around Verdun. The fort had been lightly defended and was thought to be impregnable, but a combination of factors, including a lack of communication and coordination among the French defenders, allowed the Germans to capture it relatively easily.

The loss of Fort Douaumont was a significant blow to the French morale and a major tactical victory for the Germans. However, the fort would soon become a symbol of French determination and resilience, as the French would mount a series of counter-attacks to recapture it in the months that followed.

French Counter-attacks:

Despite the initial success of the German offensive, the French defense at Verdun remained strong, and the French troops, under the leadership of Pétain, launched a series of counter-attacks to regain lost ground. These counter-attacks were characterized by their ferocity and determination, as the French sought to drive the Germans back and recapture the forts and positions they had lost.

The French counter-attacks were supported by a massive artillery barrage, as the French artillery pounded the German positions with shells, inflicting heavy casualties and forcing the Germans to retreat in some areas. The French troops, buoyed by their success, regained several key positions and prevented the Germans from achieving a decisive breakthrough.

Stalemate and Attrition:

As the battle progressed, it became clear that neither side would achieve a quick or decisive victory. The battle devolved into a stalemate, with both sides suffering heavy casualties and making little progress. The fighting was characterized by its brutal and attritional nature, as both sides dug in and fought fiercely for every inch of ground.

The German offensive had failed to achieve its objectives of capturing Verdun quickly and decisively. The French defense, bolstered by Pétain and the determination of the

French troops, had held firm, and the Germans were unable to break through the French lines.

In conclusion, the German offensive at Verdun, which began on February 21, 1916, was a major offensive that aimed to capture the strategic fortress town of Verdun and deal a significant blow to French morale. The offensive was characterized by a massive artillery bombardment followed by a ground assault, but it soon encountered fierce resistance from the French defenders. The battle would soon devolve into a stalemate, with both sides suffering heavy casualties and making little progress. The battle would continue for months, with profound consequences for both sides and for the course of the war.

The opening bombardment: "The Storm of Steel"

The opening bombardment of the Battle of Verdun, known as "The Storm of Steel," was a relentless and devastating artillery barrage unleashed by the German forces on February 21, 1916. This bombardment was a critical component of the German offensive strategy, aimed at softening the French defenses and paving the way for a successful ground assault on the fortress town of Verdun. The intensity and ferocity of the bombardment were unprecedented, and its impact on the battlefield and the soldiers involved was profound.

Scale and Intensity:

The German artillery barrage at Verdun was one of the most intense and sustained of World War I, involving over 1,200 artillery pieces, including heavy siege guns and howitzers. The bombardment lasted for ten hours and unleashed a torrent of high-explosive and shrapnel shells on the French positions and fortifications around Verdun.

The scale and intensity of the bombardment were intended to overwhelm the French defenses and destroy enemy morale. The German artillery targeted key defensive positions, communication lines, and supply routes, aiming to disrupt and disorganize the French troops.

Destruction and Chaos:

The artillery bombardment caused widespread destruction and chaos among the French defenders. The shells destroyed trenches, bunkers, and fortifications, burying soldiers alive and rendering many positions untenable.

The constant barrage of shells also created a deafening noise and a continuous rain of steel that added to the psychological impact on the soldiers. Many soldiers described the bombardment as a "storm of steel" or a "hellish inferno," as shells exploded all around them, throwing up clouds of dirt and debris.

Psychological Impact:

The bombardment had a profound psychological impact on both the French defenders and the German attackers. For the French, the constant shelling created a sense of helplessness and fear, as they were unable to respond effectively to the overwhelming firepower of the Germans.

For the Germans, the bombardment created a sense of invincibility and superiority, as they believed that they had achieved a decisive advantage over the enemy. However, this sense of superiority would soon be challenged by the determined French defense and the brutal realities of trench warfare.

Preparation for the Ground Assault:

The artillery bombardment was intended to soften up the French defenses and create gaps in the enemy lines that could be exploited by the advancing German infantry. The Germans believed that the French defenses would be so weakened by the bombardment that they would be unable to resist the ground assault.

The bombardment was followed by a ground assault by three German armies, aiming to capture Verdun and the surrounding forts. The initial advances were swift, as the German infantry encountered little resistance in the early stages of the offensive.

Legacy and Impact:

The opening bombardment of the Battle of Verdun, "The Storm of Steel," left a lasting impact on both sides and on the course of the war. The devastation and destruction caused by the bombardment were unprecedented, and the battle would soon devolve into a brutal and attritional struggle that would exact a heavy toll on both sides.

The opening bombardment of Verdun would also come to symbolize the brutal and unforgiving nature of trench warfare, as soldiers on both sides endured the constant threat of artillery fire and the horrors of life in the trenches. The battle would continue for months, with no clear victor emerging, and would ultimately end in a stalemate that would have profound consequences for both sides.

The German Infantry Advances and Early Gains at Verdun:

After the intense artillery bombardment that characterized the opening stages of the Battle of Verdun, the German infantry launched a ground assault on the French positions. This phase of the battle was marked by swift advances and early gains for the German forces, as they sought to exploit the chaos and destruction caused by the artillery barrage.

Initial Successes:

The German infantry encountered little resistance in the early stages of the offensive, as many French positions had been severely damaged or destroyed by the artillery bombardment. This allowed the Germans to advance rapidly and capture several key positions and forts around Verdun.

One of the early successes for the Germans was the capture of Fort Douaumont, one of the largest and most heavily fortified forts around Verdun. The fort had been lightly defended and was thought to be impregnable, but a combination of factors, including a lack of communication and coordination among the French defenders, allowed the Germans to capture it relatively easily.

Breakthrough at Fleury:

Another key early gain for the Germans was the capture of the village of Fleury, which lay to the northeast of Verdun. Fleury was a strategic point on the road to Verdun, and its capture allowed the Germans to threaten the town and its surrounding forts.

The capture of Fleury was achieved through a combination of infantry assaults and artillery bombardment, which forced the French defenders to retreat. The Germans quickly consolidated their position in Fleury, using it as a base for further advances towards Verdun.

Advance on the Right Bank:

On the right bank of the Meuse River, the German forces made significant advances, capturing several villages and strategic positions. The Germans crossed the Meuse at several points, using pontoon bridges to establish a foothold on the right bank and threaten the French positions on the left bank.

The German advances on the right bank were supported by artillery and infantry attacks, which aimed to dislodge the French defenders and create a breach in the enemy lines. The Germans were able to make significant gains in this sector, further threatening the French positions around Verdun.

French Counter-attacks:

Despite the early successes of the German offensive, the French defense at Verdun remained strong, and the French troops, under the leadership of General Philippe Pétain, launched a series of counter-attacks to regain lost ground. These counter-attacks were characterized by their ferocity and determination, as the French sought to drive the Germans back and recapture the forts and positions they had lost.

The French counter-attacks were supported by a massive artillery barrage, as the French artillery pounded the German positions with shells, inflicting heavy casualties and forcing the Germans to retreat in some areas. The French troops, buoyed by their success, regained several key positions and prevented the Germans from achieving a decisive breakthrough.

In conclusion, the early stages of the Battle of Verdun were marked by swift advances and early gains for the German forces, as they sought to exploit the chaos and destruction caused by the artillery bombardment. However, the French defense remained strong, and the French troops, under the leadership of Pétain, launched a series of counter-attacks to regain lost ground. The battle would continue for months, with both sides suffering heavy casualties and making little progress, leading to a stalemate that would have profound consequences for both sides.

The French Defense at Verdun:

The French defense at Verdun, from February to December 1916, was characterized by resilience, determination, and strategic planning. Led by General Philippe Pétain, the French troops mounted a tenacious defense of the fortress town, repelling repeated German assaults and holding the line against overwhelming odds. The French defense at Verdun would become a symbol of French courage and determination, and a turning point in the battle that would eventually lead to the failure of the German offensive.

Strategic Planning and Preparation:

The French were well aware of the strategic importance of Verdun and were determined to defend it at all costs. General Pétain adopted a strategy of defense in depth, with reserves held back to counter-attack and regain lost ground.

The French also focused on strengthening the defensive fortifications around Verdun, improving communications and supply lines, and bolstering the morale and discipline of the troops.

Tactical Flexibility and Adaptability:

The French defense at Verdun was characterized by tactical flexibility and adaptability. French troops were trained to react quickly to changing battlefield conditions and to make use of the terrain to their advantage.

The French made effective use of artillery and trench warfare tactics, inflicting heavy casualties on the advancing German forces and slowing their progress.

Defense of Forts and Strongpoints:

The French defense at Verdun was centered around a series of forts and strongpoints, including Fort Douaumont and

Fort Vaux, which were among the largest and most heavily fortified in France. These forts were equipped with heavy artillery and machine guns and provided a formidable defensive position.

Despite the loss of Fort Douaumont early in the battle, the French were able to hold onto Fort Vaux and several other key positions, which played a crucial role in their defense of Verdun.

Morale and Discipline:

General Pétain placed a strong emphasis on maintaining the morale and discipline of the French troops at Verdun. He visited the front lines regularly, personally inspecting the troops and boosting their morale with speeches and encouragement.

Pétain also implemented strict discipline measures, cracking down on desertion and cowardice, to ensure that the troops remained focused and determined in the face of the enemy.

Counter-attacks and Regaining Lost Ground:

Despite the early successes of the German offensive, the French defense at Verdun remained strong, and the French troops launched a series of counter-attacks to regain lost ground. These counter-attacks were supported by a massive artillery barrage and were aimed at driving the Germans back and recapturing lost positions.

The French counter-attacks were often successful, regaining several key positions and preventing the Germans from achieving a decisive breakthrough. The French troops fought bravely and tenaciously, bolstered by their determination to defend Verdun at all costs.

In conclusion, the French defense at Verdun was characterized by resilience, determination, and strategic planning. The French troops, under the leadership of Pétain, fought bravely and tenaciously, repelling repeated German assaults and holding the line against overwhelming odds. The defense of Verdun would become a symbol of French courage and determination, and a turning point in the battle that would eventually lead to the failure of the German offensive.

Petain's arrival and organization of the defense

When General Philippe Pétain arrived at Verdun in February 1916, the situation was dire. The Germans had launched a massive offensive, and the French defenses were being rapidly overwhelmed. Pétain, however, brought with him a new sense of purpose and determination, and he quickly set about organizing the defense of Verdun in a way that would eventually turn the tide of the battle.

Assessment of the Situation:

Pétain's first task upon arriving at Verdun was to assess the situation and determine the extent of the German advance. He quickly realized that the situation was critical, with the Germans making significant gains and threatening to break through the French lines.

Pétain also recognized the importance of morale and discipline in the defense of Verdun and set about instilling a sense of purpose and determination in the French troops.

Reorganization of the Defense:

One of Pétain's first acts was to reorganize the defense of Verdun. He established a system of defense in depth, with reserves held back to counter-attack and regain lost ground.

Pétain also focused on strengthening the defensive fortifications around Verdun, improving communications and supply lines, and bolstering the morale and discipline of the troops.

Emphasis on Morale and Discipline:

Pétain placed a strong emphasis on maintaining the morale and discipline of the French troops at Verdun. He visited the front lines regularly, personally inspecting the troops and boosting their morale with speeches and encouragement.

Pétain also implemented strict discipline measures, cracking down on desertion and cowardice, to ensure that the troops remained focused and determined in the face of the enemy.

Coordination of Counter-attacks:

One of Pétain's key strategies was the coordination of counter-attacks to regain lost ground. These counter-attacks were supported by a massive artillery barrage and were aimed at driving the Germans back and recapturing lost positions.

The French counter-attacks were often successful, regaining several key positions and preventing the Germans from achieving a decisive breakthrough. Pétain's leadership and organizational skills were crucial in coordinating these counter-attacks and maintaining the momentum of the French defense.

Legacy of Pétain's Leadership:

Pétain's leadership at Verdun would become legendary, and he would be hailed as the "Lion of Verdun" for his role in organizing the defense and inspiring the French troops to victory. His leadership would have a lasting impact on the French army and on the course of the war.

In conclusion, Pétain's arrival at Verdun marked a turning point in the battle. His organization of the defense, emphasis on morale and discipline, and coordination of counter-attacks were crucial in turning the tide of the battle and preventing a German breakthrough. Pétain's leadership at Verdun would become legendary, and he would be remembered as one of the key figures in the defense of Verdun.

French Counterattacks and Attempts to Regain Lost Ground at Verdun:

As the Battle of Verdun raged on from February to December 1916, the French forces, under the leadership of General Philippe Pétain, mounted a series of counterattacks to regain lost ground and repel the German forces. These counterattacks were a critical part of the French defense strategy, aiming to maintain pressure on the Germans, recapture key positions, and ultimately turn the tide of the battle in favor of the French.

Objective and Strategy:

The primary objective of the French counterattacks was to regain control of strategic positions and forts that had been lost to the Germans in the early stages of the battle. These positions, such as Fort Douaumont and Fort Vaux, were crucial to the defense of Verdun, and their loss had been a significant blow to French morale.

The French strategy involved using artillery barrages to soften up the German positions, followed by infantry assaults to recapture the lost ground. The French also made use of trench warfare tactics, such as digging tunnels under enemy lines to plant explosives and create underground attacks.

Recapture of Fort Douaumont:

One of the most famous French counterattacks at Verdun was the recapture of Fort Douaumont. The fort had been captured by the Germans in the early stages of the battle, but French forces, led by Colonel Émile Driant, launched a daring assault to retake the fort on May 22, 1916.

The French assault on Fort Douaumont was successful, and the fort was retaken after several hours of fierce fighting. The recapture of Fort Douaumont was a major morale boost for the French forces and demonstrated their determination to defend Verdun at all costs.

Counterattacks on the Right Bank:

On the right bank of the Meuse River, the French forces launched several counterattacks to regain lost ground and push the Germans back. These counterattacks were aimed at recapturing villages and strategic positions that had been captured by the Germans in the early stages of the battle.

The French counterattacks on the right bank were often successful, regaining several key positions and preventing the Germans from achieving a decisive breakthrough. The French troops fought bravely and tenaciously, bolstered by their determination to defend Verdun.

Artillery Support and Coordination:

The success of the French counterattacks was often due to the effective use of artillery support and coordination. The French artillery would soften up the German positions with a barrage of shells, creating gaps in the enemy lines that could be exploited by the advancing infantry.

The coordination between the artillery and infantry was crucial, as the timing of the assault had to be precise to maximize the impact of the artillery barrage and ensure the success of the attack.

Impact and Legacy:

The French counterattacks at Verdun were crucial in maintaining the momentum of the French defense and preventing a German breakthrough. The success of these counterattacks boosted French morale and demonstrated the determination of the French forces to defend Verdun at all costs.

The French counterattacks at Verdun would have a lasting impact on the course of the battle and the outcome of the war. The determination and resilience of the French forces would ultimately lead to the failure of the German offensive and the eventual victory of the Allies in World War I.

The Battle of Attrition

The Battle of Verdun, often referred to as the "Battle of Attrition," was characterized by its brutal and protracted nature, as both sides engaged in a relentless struggle for control of the strategic fortress town. Lasting from February to December 1916, the battle became a symbol of the horrors of trench warfare and the futility of the tactics employed by both sides.

Constant Artillery Barrages:

Throughout the battle, both the German and French forces subjected each other to constant artillery barrages, unleashing a relentless storm of shells on the enemy positions. The artillery bombardments caused widespread destruction and devastation, turning the battlefield into a desolate moonscape of craters and ruins.

The constant artillery barrages also took a heavy toll on the soldiers, both physically and mentally, as they endured the constant threat of death and destruction from above.

Trench Warfare and Stalemate:

The battle at Verdun quickly devolved into a stalemate, as both sides dug in and fortified their positions, creating a complex network of trenches, barbed wire, and defensive works. The trenches became a living hell for the soldiers, who endured mud, filth, and constant shelling.

Despite repeated attempts by both sides to break the deadlock, neither was able to achieve a decisive breakthrough. The battle became a war of attrition, with both sides suffering heavy casualties for little gain.

Human Cost:

The Battle of Verdun exacted a heavy human cost on both sides, with estimates of casualties ranging from 700,000 to over 1 million. The battle became a meat grinder, consuming the lives of countless soldiers and leaving behind a trail of death and destruction.

The human cost of the battle was compounded by the psychological toll it took on the soldiers, many of whom suffered from shell shock and other mental health issues as a result of their experiences on the battlefield.

Failure of the German Offensive:

Despite initial gains, the German offensive at Verdun ultimately failed to achieve its objectives. The French defense, led by General Philippe Pétain, proved resilient and determined, and the Germans were unable to break through the French lines.

The failure of the German offensive at Verdun was a significant blow to German morale and military prestige, and it marked a turning point in the battle, as the French began to regain lost ground and push the Germans back.

End of the Battle:

The Battle of Verdun finally came to an end in December 1916, with both sides exhausted and depleted. The battle had achieved little in terms of strategic gain, but it had exacted a heavy toll on both sides and had become a symbol of the futility and horror of war.

The Battle of Verdun would go down in history as one of the bloodiest and most brutal battles of World War I, a testament to the senseless destruction and suffering caused by war.

The Struggle for Fort Douaumont and Fort Vaux at Verdun:

Fort Douaumont and Fort Vaux were two key forts that played a crucial role in the Battle of Verdun. Both forts were heavily fortified and strategically located, making them prime targets for both the German and French forces. The struggle for control of these forts would become a focal point of the battle, with both sides fighting fiercely to gain the upper hand.

Capture of Fort Douaumont:

Fort Douaumont was the first fort to fall during the Battle of Verdun, captured by the Germans on February 25, 1916, just days after the start of the battle. The capture of Fort Douaumont was a major blow to French morale and a significant tactical victory for the Germans.

The capture of Fort Douaumont was achieved through a combination of factors, including a lack of communication and coordination among the French defenders, as well as the overwhelming firepower of the German artillery barrage.

French Attempts to Recapture Fort Douaumont:

After the loss of Fort Douaumont, the French made several attempts to recapture the fort. One of the most famous of these attempts was the counterattack on May 22, 1916, led by Colonel Émile Driant. The French assault was initially successful, but they were unable to hold onto the fort and were forced to retreat.

The French would make several more attempts to recapture Fort Douaumont in the months that followed, but all were ultimately unsuccessful. The fort remained in German hands for the duration of the battle.

Defense of Fort Vaux:

Fort Vaux, another key fortification at Verdun, also came under heavy attack from the Germans. The fort was defended by a garrison of French troops under the command of Major Sylvain-Eugène Raynal, who fought bravely to repel the German assaults.

The defense of Fort Vaux was characterized by its tenacity and determination, as the French troops endured constant shelling and attacks from the Germans. Despite being cut off from resupply and reinforcements, the garrison held out for several months before finally surrendering on June 7, 1916.

Significance of the Forts:

The struggle for Fort Douaumont and Fort Vaux was symbolic of the larger battle at Verdun, as both sides fought fiercely for control of these key positions. The forts provided valuable observation points and defensive positions, and their loss would have been a significant blow to either side.

The defense of Fort Vaux, in particular, became a symbol of French determination and resilience, as the garrison held out against overwhelming odds for an extended period of time.

Legacy:

The struggle for Fort Douaumont and Fort Vaux would go down in history as some of the most intense and brutal fighting of the Battle of Verdun. The forts would become symbols of the horrors of trench warfare and the determination of the soldiers who fought and died there.

The forts would also become lasting memorials to the soldiers who fought and died there, serving as reminders of the sacrifices made during one of the bloodiest battles of World War I.

High casualties and the relentless nature of the fighting

High casualties and the relentless nature of the fighting were defining characteristics of the Battle of Verdun. Lasting from February to December 1916, the battle resulted in staggering numbers of casualties on both sides and was marked by its brutal and unyielding nature.

Scale of Casualties:

The Battle of Verdun resulted in an estimated 700,000 to 1 million casualties, including killed, wounded, and missing. Both the French and German armies suffered immense losses, with entire regiments being decimated in the fighting.

The high casualties were a result of the relentless artillery bombardments, machine gun fire, and infantry assaults that characterized the battle. The narrow confines of the battlefield and the fortified nature of the positions made it difficult for either side to make significant gains without suffering heavy losses.

Relentless Nature of the Fighting:

The fighting at Verdun was relentless, with both sides engaged in a continuous struggle for control of key positions and fortifications. The battle devolved into a war of attrition, with neither side able to achieve a decisive breakthrough.

The narrow front and the heavily fortified nature of the positions made it difficult for either side to maneuver or outflank the enemy, leading to a series of bloody and costly frontal assaults.

Trench Warfare and Stalemate:

The Battle of Verdun epitomized the horrors of trench warfare, with soldiers on both sides enduring unimaginable hardships in the trenches. The constant threat of artillery fire, sniper attacks, and gas attacks made life in the trenches a living hell for the soldiers.

The stalemate at Verdun was a result of the entrenched positions of both sides, with neither able to dislodge the other despite repeated attempts. The battle became a war of attrition, with each side hoping to wear down the other through sheer force of will.

Impact on Soldiers:

The relentless nature of the fighting took a heavy toll on the soldiers involved, both physically and mentally. Many soldiers suffered from shell shock and other psychological traumas as a result of their experiences on the battlefield.

The high casualties and the relentless nature of the fighting at Verdun would have a lasting impact on the soldiers who fought there, as well as on the societies they came from. The battle would become a symbol of the senseless destruction and futility of war.

Legacy:

The Battle of Verdun would go down in history as one of the bloodiest and most brutal battles of World War I. It would become a symbol of the horrors of trench warfare and the high cost of war in terms of human life.

The battle would also have a lasting impact on the course of the war, as the high casualties suffered by both sides would weaken their ability to continue fighting on other fronts. The battle would ultimately end in a stalemate, with neither side able to claim a decisive victory.

The Battle in the Air and on the Ground

The Battle of Verdun witnessed not only intense fighting on the ground but also a significant aerial battle in the skies above. Both the French and German air forces played crucial roles in supporting their respective ground forces and conducting reconnaissance missions. Here is a detailed look at the battle in the air and on the ground:

Aerial Reconnaissance:

Aerial reconnaissance played a vital role in the Battle of Verdun, as both sides used aircraft to gather intelligence on enemy positions and movements. Reconnaissance planes flew over the battlefield, taking photographs and reporting back to headquarters on enemy troop movements and fortifications.

The information gathered through aerial reconnaissance was crucial for planning ground offensives and directing artillery fire. Both sides relied heavily on aerial reconnaissance to gain a tactical advantage over the enemy.

Air-to-Air Combat:

The Battle of Verdun also saw intense air-to-air combat between French and German aircraft. Fighter planes were used to protect reconnaissance aircraft and to engage enemy fighters in aerial duels.

The skies above Verdun became a battleground as pilots from both sides fought for control of the air. Dogfights were common, with pilots using machine guns and other weapons to shoot down enemy planes.

Aerial Bombardment:

Both sides also used aircraft for aerial bombardment of enemy positions. Bombers were used to drop bombs on enemy trenches, fortifications, and supply lines, inflicting damage and casualties on the enemy.

The aerial bombardment was intended to soften up enemy positions and disrupt enemy communications and supply lines. It also served to demoralize the enemy troops and create chaos behind enemy lines.

Ground Assaults and Infantry Tactics:

On the ground, the Battle of Verdun was characterized by brutal and relentless infantry assaults. Both sides used traditional infantry tactics, including frontal assaults and trench warfare, to gain ground and push the enemy back.

The narrow front and heavily fortified nature of the positions made it difficult for either side to make significant gains. The battle devolved into a war of attrition, with both sides suffering heavy casualties for little gain.

Artillery Barrages:

Artillery played a crucial role in the Battle of Verdun, with both sides using heavy artillery barrages to soften up enemy positions before infantry assaults. The constant shelling created a moonscape of craters and rubble, making movement difficult for both sides.

The artillery barrages also took a heavy toll on the soldiers, both physically and mentally, as they endured the constant threat of death and destruction from above.

In conclusion, the Battle of Verdun was a complex and multifaceted battle that involved intense fighting both in the air and on the ground. The battle was characterized by its brutality and relentless nature, as both sides fought fiercely for control of key positions and fortifications. The battle would ultimately end in a stalemate, with neither side able to achieve a decisive victory.

The role of artillery and air power in the battle

The Battle of Verdun was marked by the significant role played by artillery and air power, which had a profound impact on the course and outcome of the battle. Both sides utilized these assets extensively, showcasing the evolution of warfare during World War I.

Artillery:

Artillery played a central role in the Battle of Verdun, with both the French and German forces employing heavy artillery barrages to devastating effect. The sheer volume of artillery fire was unprecedented, leading to widespread destruction and casualties.

The artillery barrages were used to soften enemy defenses, destroy fortifications, and disrupt enemy communications and supply lines. The constant shelling created a desolate and cratered landscape, making movement difficult for infantry forces on both sides.

Artillery tactics evolved during the battle, with the introduction of new techniques such as "creeping barrages" and "counter-battery fire." Creeping barrages involved a moving curtain of artillery fire that preceded advancing infantry, while counter-battery fire targeted enemy artillery positions to suppress enemy fire.

Air Power:

Air power played an increasingly important role in the Battle of Verdun, as both sides used aircraft for reconnaissance, aerial combat, and aerial bombardment. Reconnaissance aircraft were used to gather intelligence on enemy positions and movements, while fighter planes engaged in aerial duels to gain control of the skies.

Bomber aircraft were used to conduct aerial bombardment of enemy positions, dropping bombs on enemy trenches, fortifications, and supply lines. The use of aircraft for aerial bombardment was a new and terrifying development in warfare, as it allowed for attacks on enemy positions from above.

The Battle of Verdun also saw the use of observation balloons, which were used to spot enemy positions and direct artillery fire. These balloons were vulnerable to enemy fire and were often targeted by enemy aircraft.

Impact on the Battle:

The role of artillery and air power in the Battle of Verdun was immense, as they helped shape the course and outcome of the battle. The constant artillery barrages and aerial bombardment created a hellish environment for the soldiers on the ground, leading to high casualties and psychological trauma.

The use of artillery and air power also had a profound impact on the tactics and strategies employed by both sides. The reliance on heavy artillery barrages and aerial bombardment led to a war of attrition, with both sides suffering heavy casualties for little gain.

Despite the devastating impact of artillery and air power, neither side was able to achieve a decisive breakthrough at

Verdun. The battle ultimately ended in a stalemate, with both sides exhausted and depleted.

In conclusion, the Battle of Verdun showcased the evolving nature of warfare during World War I, with the prominent role played by artillery and air power. The relentless artillery barrages and aerial bombardment created a devastating and brutal battlefield, highlighting the destructive power of modern warfare.

Infantry tactics and the experience of frontline soldiers

Infantry tactics and the experience of frontline soldiers during the Battle of Verdun were shaped by the unique challenges of trench warfare and the brutal nature of the fighting. Here is a detailed look at infantry tactics and the experience of frontline soldiers:

Trench Warfare:

Trench warfare dominated the Battle of Verdun, with both sides digging elaborate networks of trenches, bunkers, and defensive fortifications. These trenches provided cover from enemy fire but also subjected soldiers to harsh living conditions, including mud, rats, and disease.

Infantry tactics in trench warfare focused on defending and attacking trench lines. Soldiers would occupy frontline trenches, with support trenches and reserve units positioned behind them. Attacks were often preceded by artillery barrages and supported by machine gun fire.

Frontline Conditions:

Life in the trenches was grueling and exhausting for frontline soldiers. They endured constant shelling, sniper fire, and the ever-present threat of gas attacks. The trenches were often flooded with mud and water, and soldiers had to contend with lice, rats, and other vermin.

Frontline soldiers faced immense physical and mental stress, with many suffering from shell shock and other psychological traumas as a result of their experiences on the battlefield. The constant danger and death around them took a heavy toll on morale.

Infantry Tactics:

Infantry tactics at Verdun were characterized by the use of small-unit tactics, such as patrols and raids, to gather intelligence and harass the enemy. These tactics were crucial for maintaining pressure on the enemy and keeping them off balance.

The use of grenades, flamethrowers, and other close-quarters weapons was common in the trenches, as soldiers engaged in brutal hand-to-hand combat with the enemy. Bayonet charges were also used to break enemy lines and capture enemy positions.

Experience of Frontline Soldiers:

For frontline soldiers, life was a constant struggle for survival. They endured long periods of boredom and monotony interspersed with moments of intense combat and fear. Many soldiers developed close bonds with their comrades, relying on each other for support and camaraderie.

The experience of frontline soldiers was marked by a sense of duty and sacrifice, as they endured unimaginable hardships for the sake of their country and their comrades. Many soldiers faced the prospect of death on a daily basis, yet they continued to fight on, motivated by a sense of loyalty and patriotism.

Legacy:

The experience of frontline soldiers at Verdun would have a lasting impact on the soldiers themselves, as well as on the societies they came from. The horrors of trench warfare and the brutal nature of the fighting would shape the memory of the battle for generations to come.

The sacrifice and valor of the frontline soldiers at Verdun would be remembered and commemorated, serving as a reminder of the human cost of war and the resilience of the human spirit in the face of adversity.

The French Victory and Its Cost

The Battle of Verdun, often described as the "hell of Verdun," ended as a French victory, but the cost was staggering. Lasting from February to December 1916, the battle resulted in immense human suffering and loss on both sides. Here is a detailed look at the French victory and its cost:

French Victory:

The French victory at Verdun was a result of several factors, including the resilience and determination of the French soldiers, the leadership of General Philippe Pétain, and the failure of the German offensive to achieve its objectives.

The French defense at Verdun held firm, despite heavy losses and relentless German attacks. The French troops, supported by artillery and air power, were able to repel the German assaults and regain lost ground.

The turning point of the battle came in the summer of 1916, when the French launched a series of counterattacks that pushed the Germans back and eventually led to the recapture of Fort Douaumont and Fort Vaux.

Cost of Victory:

The cost of victory at Verdun was immense, with both sides suffering heavy casualties. Estimates of the total casualties vary, but it is believed that between 700,000 and 1 million men were killed, wounded, or went missing during the battle.

The French suffered approximately 377,000 casualties, including 162,000 killed or missing. The Germans suffered approximately 337,000 casualties, including 143,000 killed or missing.

The human cost of the battle was compounded by the physical and psychological toll it took on the soldiers. Many soldiers suffered from shell shock and other mental health issues as a result of their experiences on the battlefield.

Impact on the War:

The French victory at Verdun was a significant morale boost for the Allies and a blow to German prestige. The battle demonstrated the resilience of the French army and its ability to withstand a major offensive.

The battle also had strategic implications for the war, as the failure of the German offensive at Verdun weakened the German army and forced them to commit more resources to the Western Front, which ultimately contributed to the stalemate on the Western Front.

Legacy:

The Battle of Verdun would go down in history as one of the bloodiest and most brutal battles of World War I. It would become a symbol of the horrors of trench warfare and the futility of the tactics employed by both sides.

The sacrifice and valor of the soldiers who fought at Verdun would be remembered and commemorated, serving as a reminder of the human cost of war and the resilience of the human spirit in the face of adversity.

In conclusion, the French victory at Verdun came at a tremendous cost, with hundreds of thousands of men losing their lives or suffering life-changing injuries. The battle would leave a lasting impact on those who fought there and on the course of the war itself, serving as a stark reminder of the brutality and senselessness of war.

The German decision to end the offensive

The German decision to end the offensive at Verdun marked a significant turning point in the Battle of Verdun and the wider context of World War I. The decision was influenced by a variety of factors, including strategic considerations, logistical challenges, and the mounting casualties suffered by the German army.

Strategic Stalemate:

By the summer of 1916, the Battle of Verdun had reached a strategic stalemate, with neither side able to achieve a decisive breakthrough. The French defense, bolstered by reinforcements and supplies, had successfully repelled the German offensive and regained lost ground.

The failure to make significant gains at Verdun led German military commanders to reassess the strategic value of continuing the offensive. The high casualties suffered by the German army also played a role in the decision to end the offensive.

Logistical Challenges:

The logistical challenges of sustaining the offensive at Verdun were significant. The terrain was difficult, with narrow roads and limited transport infrastructure making it difficult to supply and reinforce the front lines.

The German army also faced challenges in maintaining its troops' morale and fighting effectiveness. The constant shelling, harsh living conditions, and heavy casualties took a toll on the soldiers, leading to exhaustion and low morale.

Mounting Casualties:

The Battle of Verdun had already exacted a heavy toll on the German army, with estimates of German casualties ranging from 337,000 to over 400,000. The high casualties, combined with the lack of significant gains, made it increasingly difficult to justify continuing the offensive.

The German army was also facing mounting casualties on other fronts, particularly on the Eastern Front, where they were engaged in a costly campaign against Russian forces.

Strategic Realignment:

The decision to end the offensive at Verdun marked a strategic realignment for the German army. Instead of focusing on a decisive breakthrough on the Western Front, German commanders shifted their focus to a more defensive strategy, aimed at holding their existing positions and conserving their strength.

This strategic realignment would have far-reaching consequences for the course of the war, as it marked the beginning of a period of relative stalemate on the Western Front, with neither side able to achieve a decisive victory.

In conclusion, the German decision to end the offensive at Verdun was driven by a combination of strategic, logistical, and manpower considerations. The failure to achieve a decisive breakthrough, combined with the mounting casualties and logistical challenges, led German military commanders to reassess their strategy and shift towards a more defensive posture. The decision marked a significant turning point in the Battle of Verdun and the wider context of World War I.

Assessment of the strategic outcome and impact on both sides

The Battle of Verdun had a profound strategic outcome and impact on both the French and German armies, as well as on the wider context of World War I. Here is an assessment of the strategic outcome and impact on both sides:

French Perspective:

From the French perspective, the victory at Verdun was a significant morale booster and a demonstration of the resilience and determination of the French army. The successful defense of Verdun helped restore French confidence after the setbacks of earlier battles.

The French victory at Verdun also had strategic implications, as it forced the Germans to commit more resources to the Western Front and diverted attention from other fronts. This helped relieve pressure on the Allies and contributed to the overall war effort.

German Perspective:

For the Germans, the failure to achieve a decisive breakthrough at Verdun was a major strategic setback. The high casualties suffered by the German army, combined with the lack of significant gains, led to a reassessment of German strategy on the Western Front.

The decision to end the offensive at Verdun marked a shift towards a more defensive posture for the German army, as they sought to consolidate their gains and conserve their strength. This would have long-term implications for the course of the war.

Impact on the War:

The Battle of Verdun had a significant impact on the course of the war, both militarily and psychologically. The battle demonstrated the futility of large-scale offensives and the effectiveness of trench warfare, leading to a period of relative stalemate on the Western Front.

The high casualties and brutal nature of the fighting at Verdun also had a profound psychological impact on both sides. The battle became a symbol of the horrors of war and the human cost of conflict, shaping the memory of the war for generations to come.

Legacy:

The Battle of Verdun would go down in history as one of the bloodiest and most brutal battles of World War I, a testament to the senseless destruction and suffering caused by war. The sacrifice and valor of the soldiers who fought at Verdun would be remembered and commemorated, serving as a reminder of the human cost of war.

The strategic outcome of the Battle of Verdun would have far-reaching consequences for the rest of the war, as both sides adjusted their strategies in response to the lessons learned at Verdun. The battle would ultimately shape the course of the war and the post-war settlement.

Legacy and Remembrance

The legacy of the Battle of Verdun is profound, shaping not only the course of World War I but also the collective memory of the conflict and its impact on future generations.

The battle's legacy is reflected in its remembrance, commemoration, and the lessons learned from its brutality and human cost.

Symbol of the Great War:

The Battle of Verdun has come to symbolize the horrors of World War I. It epitomizes the senseless destruction and loss of life that characterized the war, with hundreds of thousands of soldiers from both sides perishing in a brutal and protracted battle.

The battle's legacy is a stark reminder of the human cost of war and the toll it takes on individuals, families, and societies. It serves as a cautionary tale of the consequences of conflict and the importance of striving for peace.

Remembrance and Commemoration:

The Battle of Verdun is remembered and commemorated through various means, including memorials, museums, and ceremonies. The Douaumont Ossuary, containing the remains of thousands of unidentified soldiers, stands as a somber reminder of the battle's human cost.

Annually, on the anniversary of the battle, ceremonies are held to honor the fallen and to reflect on the lessons of Verdun. These ceremonies serve as a reminder of the sacrifice and valor of those who fought at Verdun and in wars since.

Lessons Learned:

The Battle of Verdun taught valuable lessons about the nature of modern warfare. It demonstrated the futility of large-scale offensives and the effectiveness of entrenched defenses, leading to a reevaluation of military strategies and tactics.

Verdun also highlighted the importance of leadership, logistics, and morale in sustaining a prolonged campaign.

The lessons learned at Verdun would influence military thinking and planning for future conflicts.

Impact on Society:

The legacy of the Battle of Verdun extends beyond the battlefield, shaping the societies that experienced the war. The battle left a deep scar on the French and German nations, impacting their collective memory and shaping their views on war and peace.

The battle's legacy is reflected in the literature, art, and culture of the time, with many artists and writers drawing inspiration from the horrors of Verdun. The battle's legacy is a reminder of the need to strive for peace and to learn from the mistakes of the past.

In conclusion, the legacy of the Battle of Verdun is multifaceted, encompassing its impact on the course of World War I, its remembrance and commemoration, and the lessons learned from its brutality and human cost. The battle's legacy serves as a reminder of the human cost of war and the importance of striving for peace and understanding in a world scarred by conflict.

Commemoration of the battle and its significance in French history

The Battle of Verdun holds significant importance in French history and is commemorated in various ways to honor the memory of those who fought and died in one of the bloodiest battles of World War I. The commemoration of the battle is a reminder of the sacrifices made by the French soldiers and the resilience of the French nation in the face of adversity.

Douaumont Ossuary and Cemetery:

The Douaumont Ossuary is a central site for the commemoration of the Battle of Verdun. It contains the remains of over 130,000 unidentified soldiers who perished in the battle. The ossuary serves as a solemn reminder of the human cost of war and a place of remembrance for the fallen.

The Douaumont Cemetery, located nearby, is the final resting place for thousands of French soldiers who died at Verdun. The cemetery is meticulously maintained and is a place of pilgrimage for those wishing to pay their respects to the fallen.

Commemorative Ceremonies:

Annually, on the anniversary of the battle, commemorative ceremonies are held at Verdun to honor the memory of the soldiers who fought and died there. These ceremonies include wreath-laying ceremonies, military parades, and speeches by dignitaries and military officials.

The ceremonies are attended by veterans, descendants of soldiers who fought at Verdun, and representatives from the French government and military. They serve as a reminder of the sacrifice and valor of those who fought at Verdun and the importance of remembering their legacy.

Memorials and Monuments:

Throughout the Verdun region, there are numerous memorials and monuments dedicated to the Battle of Verdun and the soldiers who fought there. These monuments serve as reminders of the battle's significance in French history and its impact on the nation.

One of the most famous monuments is the "Monument to the Dead" in Verdun, which lists the names of over 150,000 French soldiers who died at Verdun. The monument is a powerful symbol of remembrance and a testament to the scale of the sacrifice made by the French nation.

Educational and Cultural Significance:

The Battle of Verdun is also commemorated through educational programs, exhibitions, and cultural events that highlight its significance in French history. These programs seek to educate the public about the battle and its impact on French society and culture.

The battle's legacy is also reflected in literature, art, and music, with many artists and writers drawing inspiration from the horrors of Verdun. These works serve as a reminder of the human cost of war and the need to strive for peace and understanding.

In conclusion, the commemoration of the Battle of Verdun is a solemn and significant event in French history, honoring the memory of those who fought and died in one of the most brutal battles of World War I. The commemoration serves as a reminder of the sacrifice and valor of the French soldiers and the resilience of the French nation in the face of adversity.

Lessons learned from Verdun for future military planning

The Battle of Verdun provided several important lessons for future military planning, particularly in terms of strategy, tactics, and the conduct of warfare. These lessons have had a lasting impact on military thinking and continue to influence military planning to this day.

Trench Warfare and Static Fronts:

Verdun highlighted the effectiveness of entrenched defenses and the challenges of attacking well-fortified positions. It demonstrated the importance of integrating infantry, artillery, and air power to overcome entrenched defenses.

The battle showed that frontal assaults against fortified positions could result in high casualties and minimal gains, leading to a reassessment of offensive strategies on static fronts.

Importance of Logistics and Support:

The logistical challenges faced by both sides at Verdun underscored the importance of logistics and support in sustaining a prolonged campaign. The battle demonstrated the need for effective supply lines and support services to maintain troop morale and effectiveness.

Military planners learned the importance of planning for sustained operations, including the need for adequate supplies of ammunition, food, and medical support.

Role of Artillery and Air Power:

Verdun highlighted the crucial role played by artillery and air power in modern warfare. The battle showed that artillery could be used not only to soften enemy defenses but also to provide close support for infantry assaults.

The use of aircraft for reconnaissance and aerial bombardment was also demonstrated at Verdun, showing the potential for air power to influence the outcome of a battle.

Human Cost of War:

Perhaps the most enduring lesson of Verdun is the human cost of war. The battle resulted in hundreds of thousands of casualties and left a lasting impact on the soldiers who fought there.

The battle served as a stark reminder of the horrors of war and the need to strive for peace. It highlighted the importance of minimizing civilian casualties and protecting non-combatants during armed conflict.

Adaptability and Flexibility:

Verdun showed the importance of adaptability and flexibility in military planning. Both sides had to constantly adapt their strategies and tactics in response to changing battlefield conditions.

Military planners learned the importance of having a flexible and responsive command structure, capable of adjusting to unforeseen challenges and opportunities on the battlefield.

In conclusion, the Battle of Verdun provided several important lessons for future military planning, including the importance of entrenched defenses, the role of logistics and support, the effectiveness of artillery and air power, and the human cost of war. These lessons have had a lasting impact on military thinking and continue to shape military planning and strategy today.

The Battle of the Somme: A Costly Offensive

Introduction

The Battle of the Somme, fought from July to November 1916, stands as one of the most iconic and tragic battles of World War I. Planned as a joint British and French offensive against the German Army on the Western Front, the battle aimed to achieve a breakthrough and relieve pressure on the French forces at Verdun. However, the Battle of the Somme would instead become synonymous with the horrors of trench warfare and the staggering human cost of industrialized warfare.

The battle's origins can be traced back to the strategic situation on the Western Front in 1916. The French Army, under immense pressure at Verdun, called upon their British allies to launch a diversionary offensive along the Somme River. The British Army, under the command of General Sir Douglas Haig, agreed to the plan and began preparations for a major offensive in the summer of 1916.

The Battle of the Somme was preceded by a week-long artillery bombardment, intended to soften up the German defenses and destroy their barbed wire entanglements. However, the effectiveness of the bombardment was limited, as the Germans had constructed deep and well-fortified defensive positions. When the British and French forces launched their assault on July 1st, they were met with fierce resistance and heavy casualties.

The first day of the Battle of the Somme remains the bloodiest day in the history of the British Army, with over 57,000 casualties, including nearly 20,000 killed. Despite these staggering losses, the British and French forces continued to press forward, hoping to achieve a breakthrough and advance towards the German lines.

The battle soon devolved into a brutal and protracted stalemate, with both sides suffering heavy casualties and making little progress. The fighting was characterized by brutal hand-to-hand combat, as soldiers fought for control of small patches of ground at a staggering cost in lives.

The Battle of the Somme also saw the first widespread use of new weapons and tactics that would come to define World War I. The use of tanks, although still in its infancy, provided a glimpse of the future of armored warfare. Similarly, the use of aircraft for reconnaissance and ground attack marked a new era in military aviation.

As the battle dragged on into the autumn months, the weather deteriorated, turning the battlefield into a muddy quagmire. The harsh conditions made movement and resupply difficult, further adding to the misery of the soldiers on both sides.

By the time the Battle of the Somme finally came to an end in November 1916, the British and French forces had advanced only a few miles and suffered over 600,000 casualties. The German Army, while also suffering heavy losses, had managed to hold their ground and prevent a decisive breakthrough.

In the end, the Battle of the Somme did not achieve its intended objectives of breaking the German lines or relieving pressure on Verdun. Instead, it became a symbol of the futility and horror of war, with hundreds of thousands of young men sacrificing their lives in a brutal and senseless conflict

Today, the Battle of the Somme is remembered as a defining moment in World War I, a testament to the courage and sacrifice of the soldiers who fought there. The battle serves as a reminder of the human cost of war and the importance of remembering those who gave their lives in the pursuit of peace.

Setting the Stage for the battle

Setting the stage for the Battle of the Somme involved a complex interplay of military, political, and strategic factors that culminated in one of the largest and bloodiest battles of World War I. The battle took place in the Somme region of northern France, along a 25-mile front, and lasted from July to November 1916. Here's how the stage was set for this monumental clash:

Strategic Situation:

By 1916, the war on the Western Front had reached a stalemate, with neither side able to achieve a decisive breakthrough. The French were under intense pressure at Verdun, where they were engaged in a desperate battle to repel a German offensive.

The British, eager to relieve pressure on their French allies, planned a major offensive along the Somme River. The objective was to achieve a breakthrough, advance into German-held territory, and ultimately force the Germans to divert troops from Verdun.

Preparations and Planning:

The British Army, under the command of General Sir Douglas Haig, began preparations for the offensive in early 1916. Extensive artillery bombardments were planned to soften up the German defenses and destroy their barbed wire entanglements.

The British also made use of new weapons and tactics, including tanks and improved artillery techniques, in an attempt to overcome the formidable German defenses.

German Defenses:

The Germans had constructed a series of deep and well-fortified defensive positions along the Somme front. These defenses included trenches, bunkers, and machine gun emplacements, as well as extensive barbed wire entanglements.

The Germans were well-prepared for the British offensive and had made extensive use of their time in the winter and spring of 1916 to fortify their positions and prepare for the coming battle.

The Opening Barrage:

On July 1, 1916, the British launched their long-awaited offensive with a massive artillery bombardment. The bombardment was intended to destroy the German defenses and create a path for the advancing infantry.

However, the effectiveness of the bombardment was limited, as the Germans had constructed deep dugouts and shelters to protect their troops. When the infantry went over the top, they were met with fierce resistance and heavy casualties.

Initial Advances and Stalemate:

Despite heavy losses, the British and French forces managed to make some initial gains in the opening days of the battle. However, progress soon ground to a halt as the Germans brought up reinforcements and strengthened their defenses.

The battle devolved into a brutal and protracted stalemate, with both sides suffering heavy casualties and making little progress. The fighting would continue for months, resulting in hundreds of thousands of casualties on both sides.

In conclusion, the stage was set for the Battle of the Somme by a combination of strategic objectives, meticulous planning, and the harsh realities of trench warfare. The battle would ultimately become a symbol of the futility and horror of war, with both sides enduring unimaginable suffering in a conflict that would leave a lasting impact on the course of World War I.

Background to the Battle of the Somme

The background to the Battle of the Somme is rooted in the strategic and military developments of World War I up to 1916. The battle was influenced by a combination of factors, including the strategic situation on the Western Front, the military objectives of the Allies, and the evolving nature of warfare.

Stalemate on the Western Front:

By 1916, the war on the Western Front had reached a stalemate, with both the Allies and the Central Powers unable to achieve a decisive breakthrough. Trench warfare had become the dominant form of combat, characterized by static defensive positions and costly frontal assaults.

The Allies, particularly the British and French, were eager to break the deadlock and achieve a breakthrough that would lead to a decisive victory.

French Situation at Verdun:

In early 1916, the German Army launched a major offensive against the French fortress of Verdun. The French Army, under intense pressure, fought desperately to defend the fortress and prevent a German breakthrough.

The situation at Verdun placed enormous strain on the French Army and raised concerns among the Allies about the ability of the French to continue the fight.

British Plans for an Offensive:

The British, under the command of General Sir Douglas Haig, planned a major offensive in the summer of 1916 to relieve pressure on the French at Verdun and break the stalemate on the Western Front.

The objective of the offensive was to achieve a breakthrough along the Somme River, advance into German-held territory, and ultimately force the Germans to divert troops from Verdun.

Preparations for the Offensive:

The British Army made extensive preparations for the offensive, including the stockpiling of artillery shells, the construction of trenches and dugouts, and the training of troops in new tactics and techniques.

The British also planned to make use of new weapons, including tanks, in an attempt to overcome the formidable German defenses.

German Defensive Preparations:

The Germans were aware of the Allied plans for an offensive along the Somme and made extensive preparations to defend their positions. They constructed a series of deep and well-fortified defensive positions, including trenches, bunkers, and machine gun emplacements.

The Germans also made use of barbed wire entanglements and other obstacles to impede the advance of Allied troops.

In conclusion, the background to the Battle of the Somme was shaped by the strategic and military developments of World War I up to 1916. The battle was a response to the stalemate on the Western Front, the French situation at Verdun, and the British plans for a major offensive. The battle would ultimately become one of the largest and bloodiest battles of World War I, with profound consequences for the course of the war.

Objectives and strategies of the British and French forces

The Battle of the Somme was a key offensive launched by the British and French forces on the Western Front during World War I. The objectives and strategies of the British and French forces were shaped by the need to relieve pressure on the French at Verdun, break the stalemate on the Western Front, and achieve a decisive breakthrough against the German Army. Here's a detailed look at their objectives and strategies:

British Objectives:

The primary objective of the British was to achieve a breakthrough along the Somme River and advance into German-held territory. This would relieve pressure on the French at Verdun and potentially lead to a decisive victory on the Western Front.

The British also hoped to draw German reserves away from other sectors of the front, weakening the overall German position and creating opportunities for further offensives.

British Strategy:

The British strategy for the Battle of the Somme was based on a massive artillery bombardment followed by a coordinated infantry assault. The artillery bombardment was intended to destroy German defenses and create gaps in the enemy lines.

The British also planned to use new weapons and tactics, including tanks, to support the infantry assault and overcome German defenses. The use of tanks was still experimental at the time, but the British hoped that their introduction would give them a significant advantage on the battlefield.

French Objectives:

The French objectives at the Battle of the Somme were closely aligned with those of the British. The French aimed to achieve a breakthrough along their sector of the front and advance into German-held territory.

The French also hoped to relieve pressure on their forces at Verdun and prevent a German victory that could potentially lead to the collapse of the French Army.

French Strategy:

The French strategy for the Battle of the Somme was similar to that of the British, with a heavy emphasis on artillery bombardment and infantry assault. The French also planned to use tanks and other new weapons to support their attack.

The French coordinated closely with the British, ensuring that their offensives were timed and executed in concert to maximize the impact on the German defenses.

Overall Allied Strategy:

The overall Allied strategy for the Battle of the Somme was to launch a coordinated offensive along a wide front, stretching from the River Somme to the River Ancre. This would prevent the Germans from concentrating their defenses in any one sector and increase the likelihood of achieving a breakthrough.

The Allied forces also planned to conduct a series of limited offensives to keep the pressure on the Germans and maintain the momentum of the attack.

In conclusion, the objectives and strategies of the British and French forces at the Battle of the Somme were aimed at achieving a breakthrough on the Western Front and relieving pressure on the French at Verdun. While the battle ultimately resulted in heavy casualties and limited gains, it marked a significant turning point in the war and set the stage for future Allied offensives.

The Plan and Preparations

The plan and preparations for the Battle of the Somme were extensive and involved meticulous coordination between the British and French forces. The plan was to launch a massive offensive along a 25-mile front, with the objective of achieving a breakthrough and advancing into German-held territory. Here's a detailed look at the plan and preparations for the battle:

Artillery Bombardment:

The plan called for a week-long artillery bombardment of the German positions along the Somme front. The bombardment was intended to destroy German defenses, including trenches, bunkers, and barbed wire entanglements, and soften up the enemy for the infantry assault.

The British and French forces amassed a huge arsenal of artillery, including heavy guns and howitzers, for the bombardment. The bombardment was one of the largest in history up to that point and was intended to be a decisive factor in the battle.

Infantry Assault:

Following the artillery bombardment, the British and French infantry would advance across no man's land and assault the German positions. The infantry were to be supported by tanks, which were used for the first time in a major offensive during the battle.

The infantry assault was preceded by the detonation of a series of mines under the German lines, creating craters and disrupting the enemy defenses.

Tanks and New Weapons:

The Battle of the Somme saw the first widespread use of tanks in combat. The tanks were intended to provide support for the infantry assault and help overcome German defenses. However, many of the tanks broke down or became stuck in the mud, limiting their effectiveness.

The battle also saw the use of new weapons and tactics, including improved artillery techniques and gas attacks, aimed at breaking the deadlock on the Western Front.

Logistics and Supply:

Extensive preparations were made to ensure that the troops were adequately supplied during the battle. Supply lines were established, and stockpiles of ammunition, food, and medical supplies were built up in preparation for the offensive.

Special attention was paid to the transportation of troops and supplies, with new rail lines and roads constructed to facilitate the movement of troops to the front lines.

Training and Rehearsals:

The troops were given extensive training in the weeks leading up to the battle, with an emphasis on new tactics and techniques. Rehearsals were conducted to familiarize the troops with the plan and ensure that they were prepared for the assault.

The use of tanks and other new weapons required specialized training, and efforts were made to ensure that the troops were fully trained in their use.

In conclusion, the plan and preparations for the Battle of the Somme were extensive and involved a combination of artillery bombardment, infantry assault, and the use of new weapons and tactics. Despite the meticulous planning, the battle would ultimately result in heavy casualties and limited gains, highlighting the challenges of modern warfare on the Western Front.

The initial plans for the offensive

The initial plans for the offensive at the Battle of the Somme were ambitious and aimed at achieving a decisive breakthrough on the Western Front. The British and French forces planned to launch a massive assault along a 25-mile front, with the objective of advancing into German-held territory and relieving pressure on the French at Verdun. Here's a detailed look at the initial plans for the offensive:

Objectives:

The primary objective of the offensive was to achieve a breakthrough along the Somme front and advance into

German-held territory. This would relieve pressure on the French at Verdun and potentially lead to a decisive victory on the Western Front.

The British and French hoped to draw German reserves away from other sectors of the front, weakening the overall German position and creating opportunities for further offensives.

Timing and Coordination:

The offensive was originally planned for the summer of 1916, with the exact timing dependent on a number of factors, including the weather and the readiness of the troops.

The British and French forces coordinated closely on the timing and execution of the offensive, ensuring that their attacks were synchronized to maximize the impact on the German defenses.

Artillery Bombardment:

The plan called for a massive artillery bombardment of the German positions along the Somme front, intended to destroy enemy defenses and soften up the enemy for the infantry assault.

The artillery bombardment was to last for seven days and was one of the largest in history up to that point, involving thousands of guns and millions of shells.

Infantry Assault:

Following the artillery bombardment, the British and French infantry would advance across no man's land and assault the German positions. The infantry were to be supported by tanks, which were used for the first time in a major offensive during the battle.

The infantry assault was preceded by the detonation of a series of mines under the German lines, creating craters and disrupting the enemy defenses.

Tactics and Techniques:

The battle saw the use of new tactics and techniques, including the use of tanks, improved artillery techniques, and gas attacks, aimed at breaking the deadlock on the Western Front.

The use of tanks, although still experimental, was intended to provide the infantry with much-needed support and help overcome German defenses.

In conclusion, the initial plans for the offensive at the Battle of the Somme were ambitious and aimed at achieving a decisive breakthrough on the Western Front. Despite meticulous planning and coordination, the battle would ultimately result in heavy casualties and limited gains, highlighting the challenges of modern warfare on the Western Front.

Preparations including artillery bombardment and troop deployments

The preparations for the Battle of the Somme were extensive and involved meticulous planning and coordination between the British and French forces. The preparations included a massive artillery bombardment, troop deployments, and the construction of trenches and defensive positions. Here's a detailed look at the preparations for the battle:

Artillery Bombardment:

The artillery bombardment was a central component of the preparations for the Battle of the Somme. The bombardment was intended to destroy German defenses, including trenches, bunkers, and barbed wire entanglements, and soften up the enemy for the infantry assault.

The bombardment lasted for seven days and involved thousands of guns firing millions of shells. It was one of the largest artillery bombardments in history up to that point.

Troop Deployments:

The British and French forces deployed hundreds of thousands of troops along the Somme front in preparation for the offensive. Troops were moved into position under cover of darkness to conceal their movements from the enemy.

Special attention was paid to the deployment of infantry, artillery, and support units to ensure that they were in the right positions to support the offensive.

Trench Construction:

The British and French forces constructed a network of trenches and defensive positions in preparation for the offensive. Trenches were dug in zigzag patterns to minimize the impact of artillery fire and provide cover for the troops.

The trenches were equipped with communication trenches, dugouts, and other fortifications to protect the troops from enemy fire.

Supply and Logistics:

Extensive preparations were made to ensure that the troops were adequately supplied during the battle. Supply lines were established, and stockpiles of ammunition, food, and medical supplies were built up in preparation for the offensive.

Special attention was paid to the transportation of troops and supplies, with new rail lines and roads constructed to facilitate the movement of troops to the front lines.

Gas and Smoke Screens:

The British and French forces used gas and smoke screens to conceal their movements and confuse the enemy during the offensive. Gas attacks were also used to disrupt enemy positions and force them to wear gas masks, hampering their effectiveness.

In conclusion, the preparations for the Battle of the Somme were extensive and involved a combination of artillery bombardment, troop deployments, and the construction of defensive positions. Despite the meticulous planning, the battle would ultimately result in heavy casualties and limited gains, highlighting the challenges of modern warfare on the Western Front.

The First Day: July 1, 1916

The first day of the Battle of the Somme, July 1, 1916, is remembered as one of the darkest days in British military history. It was the day when the British Army launched its long-awaited offensive along the Somme front, with the objective of achieving a breakthrough and advancing into German-held territory. However, the day would instead become synonymous with the horrors of trench warfare and the staggering human cost of industrialized warfare.

The Artillery Barrage:

The day began with a massive artillery barrage, as thousands of British guns opened fire on the German positions along the Somme front. The barrage was intended to destroy German defenses and create gaps in the enemy lines for the infantry to exploit.

The Infantry Assault:

Following the artillery barrage, the British infantry went over the top and advanced across no man's land towards the

German lines. The infantry were supported by tanks, which were used for the first time in a major offensive during the battle.

However, the effectiveness of the artillery barrage was limited, and the German defenses proved to be more formidable than expected. The infantry encountered heavy machine gun fire and artillery barrages as they advanced, resulting in heavy casualties.

Casualties:

The first day of the Battle of the Somme remains the bloodiest day in the history of the British Army, with over 57,000 casualties, including nearly 20,000 killed. The losses were catastrophic and had a profound impact on the British Army and the nation as a whole.

The casualties were the result of a combination of factors, including the failure of the artillery barrage to destroy German defenses, the effectiveness of the German machine gun positions, and the lack of coordination between the infantry and tank units.

Limited Gains:

Despite the heavy losses, some British units managed to make limited gains on the first day of the battle. However, these gains were small and came at a high cost in lives.

The failure to achieve a decisive breakthrough on the first day of the battle set the tone for the rest of the campaign, which would devolve into a brutal and protracted stalemate.

In conclusion, the first day of the Battle of the Somme was a day of tragedy and loss for the British Army. The failure to achieve a breakthrough on the first day would set the stage for months of brutal fighting and heavy casualties, making the Battle of the Somme one of the most costly battles in British military history.

Overview of the initial attacks and objectives

The initial attacks of the Battle of the Somme were part of a larger offensive launched by the British and French forces along the Somme front on July 1, 1916. The objectives of the initial attacks were to achieve a breakthrough in the German lines, advance into German-held territory, and relieve pressure on the French forces at Verdun. Here's an overview of the initial attacks and objectives:

The Plan:

The British and French forces planned a coordinated offensive along a 25-mile front, stretching from the River Somme to the River Ancre. The objective was to achieve a breakthrough and advance into German-held territory.

The plan called for a massive artillery bombardment followed by an infantry assault supported by tanks. The infantry were to advance across no man's land and assault the German positions, with the tanks providing support and cover.

The Objectives:

The primary objective of the initial attacks was to achieve a breakthrough along the Somme front and advance into German-held territory. This would relieve pressure on the French at Verdun and potentially lead to a decisive victory on the Western Front.

The British and French also hoped to draw German reserves away from other sectors of the front, weakening the overall German position and creating opportunities for further offensives.

The Infantry Assault:

The infantry assault began after a massive artillery bombardment, during which thousands of British guns fired millions of shells at the German positions. The infantry advanced across no man's land towards the German lines, supported by tanks.

However, the effectiveness of the artillery bombardment was limited, and the German defenses proved to be more formidable than expected. The infantry encountered heavy machine gun fire and artillery barrages, resulting in heavy casualties.

Limited Gains:

Despite heavy losses, some British units managed to make limited gains on the first day of the battle. However, these gains were small and came at a high cost in lives.

The failure to achieve a decisive breakthrough on the first day set the tone for the rest of the campaign, which would devolve into a brutal and protracted stalemate.

In conclusion, the initial attacks of the Battle of the Somme were part of a larger offensive aimed at achieving a breakthrough on the Western Front. Despite meticulous planning and coordination, the initial attacks would ultimately result in heavy casualties and limited gains, highlighting the challenges of modern warfare on the Western Front.

Challenges and setbacks faced by the Allied forces

The Allied forces faced numerous challenges and setbacks during the Battle of the Somme, which hindered their ability to achieve their objectives and resulted in heavy casualties. These challenges included the formidable German defenses, the difficult terrain, logistical issues, and the weather. Here's a detailed look at the challenges and setbacks faced by the Allied forces:

Formidable German Defenses:

The German defenses along the Somme front were well-prepared and formidable, consisting of deep trenches, concrete bunkers, and extensive barbed wire entanglements.

The German defenses were further strengthened by the use of machine guns, artillery, and other weapons, which inflicted heavy casualties on the advancing Allied troops.

Difficult Terrain:

The terrain along the Somme front was difficult, with muddy and waterlogged conditions making movement difficult for both troops and equipment.

The difficult terrain hampered the Allied advance and made it difficult to establish and maintain supply lines, leading to logistical challenges.

Logistical Issues:

The scale of the offensive and the challenging terrain presented significant logistical challenges for the Allied forces. Supplying troops with ammunition, food, and medical supplies was difficult, and communication lines were often disrupted.

The use of new weapons and tactics, such as tanks, also posed logistical challenges, as they required specialized maintenance and support.

Weather Conditions:

The weather during the Battle of the Somme was often inclement, with heavy rain and mud making conditions even more challenging for the troops.

The wet and muddy conditions made movement difficult, bogging down troops and equipment and hampering the effectiveness of the artillery bombardment.

Counterattacks and Resilience of the Germans:

The Germans launched counterattacks against the Allied forces, attempting to regain lost ground and disrupt their advance.

The Germans showed great resilience and determination in defending their positions, often launching fierce counterattacks that inflicted heavy casualties on the Allied forces.

Lack of Coordination and Communication:

The Allied forces faced challenges in coordinating their attacks and communicating effectively due to the difficult terrain and the breakdown of communication lines.

This lack of coordination and communication hindered their ability to respond to changing battlefield conditions and exploit opportunities for advancement.

In conclusion, the Allied forces faced numerous challenges and setbacks during the Battle of the Somme, including formidable German defenses, difficult terrain, logistical issues, and inclement weather. These challenges hindered their ability to achieve their objectives and resulted in heavy casualties, highlighting the brutal and unforgiving nature of modern warfare on the Western Front.

Tactics and Technology

The Battle of the Somme saw the use of a variety of tactics and technologies by both the Allied and German forces as they sought to gain the upper hand on the battlefield. These tactics and technologies evolved throughout the course of the battle as both sides adapted to the challenges they faced. Here's an overview of the tactics and technology used during the Battle of the Somme:

Trench Warfare:

Trench warfare was the dominant form of combat on the Western Front during World War I, and the Battle of the Somme was no exception. Both sides dug elaborate trench systems to protect their troops from enemy fire.

Trench warfare was characterized by a static front line, with troops launching attacks across no man's land to try and gain ground. However, these attacks were often costly and resulted in heavy casualties.

Artillery Barrages:

Artillery played a crucial role in the Battle of the Somme, with both sides using massive barrages to soften up enemy defenses before launching infantry assaults.

The British and French forces fired millions of shells during the battle, but the effectiveness of the artillery was often limited by the difficult terrain and the resilience of the German defenses.

Gas Attacks:

Both sides used poison gas during the Battle of the Somme, although its effectiveness was limited by the prevailing wind conditions and the use of gas masks by the troops.

Gas attacks were intended to disrupt enemy positions and force the enemy to wear gas masks, hampering their effectiveness in combat.

Machine Guns:

Machine guns were a key weapon used by both sides during the Battle of the Somme. German machine gun positions were particularly effective at inflicting casualties on advancing Allied troops.

The use of machine guns contributed to the high casualty rates seen during the battle, as troops were often cut down as they advanced across no man's land.

Tanks:

The Battle of the Somme saw the first widespread use of tanks in combat. The British used tanks to support their infantry assaults, with mixed results.

While tanks were effective at overcoming some German defenses, they were often prone to mechanical failures and were vulnerable to enemy artillery and machine gun fire.

Aerial Reconnaissance:

Both sides used aircraft for reconnaissance purposes during the Battle of the Somme. Aircraft were used to gather intelligence on enemy positions and troop movements, helping to inform their own tactics and strategies.

Aerial reconnaissance also played a role in artillery spotting, helping to improve the accuracy of artillery fire.

In conclusion, the Battle of the Somme saw the use of a variety of tactics and technologies as both sides sought to gain the upper hand on the battlefield. While some of these tactics and technologies were effective, others were less so, highlighting the challenges of modern warfare on the Western Front.

Infantry tactics and advances in military technology

The Battle of the Somme marked a significant turning point in infantry tactics and the use of military technology during World War I. The battle saw the evolution of new tactics and the introduction of new technologies that would shape the course of the war. Here's an overview of the infantry tactics and advances in military technology during the Battle of the Somme:

Infantry Tactics:

The Battle of the Somme highlighted the limitations of traditional infantry tactics, which relied heavily on frontal assaults across no man's land.

The high casualty rates suffered by the infantry on the first day of the battle led to a reevaluation of tactics, with a greater emphasis placed on small-unit tactics, such as infiltration and use of cover.

Bayonet Charges:

Bayonet charges were a common tactic used by infantry during World War I, including at the Battle of the Somme. However, the effectiveness of bayonet charges was limited by the presence of barbed wire and machine gun fire.

Use of Grenades:

Grenades were widely used by infantry during the Battle of the Somme, both as offensive weapons to clear enemy trenches and as defensive weapons to repel enemy attacks.

The introduction of new types of grenades, such as the Mills bomb, improved the effectiveness of infantry in close-quarters combat.

Machine Gun Tactics:

Machine guns played a crucial role in the Battle of the Somme, with both sides using them to defend their positions and inflict heavy casualties on advancing infantry.

The British and French forces developed tactics to neutralize enemy machine gun positions, including the use of creeping barrages and flanking attacks.

Artillery Support:

Artillery played a key role in supporting infantry assaults during the Battle of the Somme. Artillery barrages were used to soften up enemy defenses before infantry attacks, although the effectiveness of the artillery was often limited by the difficult terrain.

Introduction of Tanks:

The Battle of the Somme saw the first widespread use of tanks in combat. Tanks were used to support infantry assaults, providing cover and firepower against enemy positions.

While the early tanks were prone to mechanical failures and were vulnerable to enemy fire, they represented a significant advance in military technology and would play a larger role in future battles.

Aerial Reconnaissance:

Aircraft were used for reconnaissance purposes during the Battle of the Somme, providing valuable intelligence on enemy positions and troop movements.

Aerial reconnaissance helped to inform infantry tactics and artillery targeting, improving the overall effectiveness of the Allied forces.

In conclusion, the Battle of the Somme saw significant advances in infantry tactics and the use of military technology. While some of these advances were more successful than others, they all contributed to the evolving nature of warfare on the Western Front during World War I.

The use of tanks for the first time in battle

The Battle of the Somme marked a historic moment in military history as it witnessed the first widespread use of tanks in battle. Tanks were a new and innovative weapon designed to break the deadlock of trench warfare and overcome the formidable defenses of the German Army. Here's an overview of the use of tanks for the first time in battle during the Battle of the Somme:

Development of Tanks:

Tanks were developed in response to the stalemate of trench warfare on the Western Front. They were designed to cross trenches, crush barbed wire, and provide mobile firepower to support infantry assaults.

The British Army developed the Mark I tank, which was the first tank to see combat. It had a crew of eight and was armed with machine guns and small cannons.

Deployment of Tanks:

On September 15, 1916, during the Battle of Flers-Courcelette, tanks were used for the first time in a major offensive. A total of 49 tanks were deployed, with mixed results.

The tanks were meant to lead the infantry assault, but many broke down or got stuck in the mud. Despite these setbacks, the tanks proved to be effective in breaking through some German defenses and causing confusion among the enemy.

Impact on the Battlefield:

The introduction of tanks had a significant impact on the battlefield. They provided a new and terrifying weapon that the Germans had not encountered before, causing panic and confusion among their ranks.

Tanks were effective at overcoming some of the obstacles of trench warfare, such as barbed wire and machine gun positions. However, their effectiveness was limited by their slow speed, mechanical unreliability, and vulnerability to artillery fire.

Evolution of Tank Tactics:

The early use of tanks at the Battle of the Somme highlighted the need for improved tactics and technology. Tanks were used in conjunction with infantry and artillery to maximize their effectiveness.

Over time, tank tactics evolved, leading to the development of more advanced tanks and tactics that would be used in future battles.

Legacy:

The use of tanks at the Battle of the Somme marked the beginning of a new era in warfare. Tanks would go on to play a major role in World War II and in conflicts thereafter, revolutionizing the way wars are fought.

In conclusion, the use of tanks for the first time in battle during the Battle of the Somme was a historic moment that changed the course of military history. While their initial deployment was not without its challenges, tanks would go on to become a key weapon on the battlefield, shaping the future of warfare.

The Battle Rages On

The Battle of the Somme was characterized by intense and prolonged fighting as both sides struggled for control of the strategically important territory. Despite heavy casualties and the challenges of trench warfare, the battle continued for months, with neither side able to achieve a decisive victory. The fighting was marked by brutal close-quarters combat, artillery barrages, and the use of new technologies such as tanks and aircraft. The Battle of the Somme would ultimately result in a stalemate, with both sides suffering tremendous losses and the front lines remaining largely unchanged.

Progress of the battle over the following months

The Battle of the Somme, which began on July 1, 1916, continued for several months, lasting until November of the same year. Over this period, the battle evolved and changed as both sides adapted their tactics and strategies. The progress of the battle over the following months was characterized by a series of offensives and counteroffensives, heavy casualties, and limited gains. Here's an overview of the progress of the battle over the following months:

July 1916:

The initial phase of the battle saw heavy fighting and high casualties, particularly on the first day, which remains one of the bloodiest days in British military history.

Despite some initial gains, particularly in the south of the battlefield, the British and French forces were unable to achieve a decisive breakthrough.

August 1916:

In August, the focus of the battle shifted to the northern part of the battlefield, where the British launched a series of offensives near the village of Guillemont and the town of Pozieres.

The fighting in August was fierce, with both sides suffering heavy casualties. The British managed to make some gains, but they were limited and came at a high cost.

September 1916:

September saw the continuation of the British offensives, with a renewed push towards the village of Flers and the introduction of new tactics and technologies, including the use of tanks.

The introduction of tanks had a limited impact on the battle, as many broke down or got stuck in the mud. However, they did help to break through some of the German defenses.

October 1916:

In October, the battle continued to grind on, with both sides suffering heavy losses and making limited gains.

The British made some progress near the village of Le Transloy, but they were unable to achieve a decisive breakthrough.

November 1916:

The Battle of the Somme finally came to an end in November, as the onset of winter weather made further offensives difficult.

By the end of the battle, the British and French forces had advanced a few miles at most along a 15-mile front, at a cost of over a million casualties.

Overall, the Battle of the Somme was a costly and inconclusive battle that failed to achieve its strategic objectives. The battle highlighted the challenges of modern warfare on the Western

Front, including the difficulty of achieving a breakthrough against well-entrenched defenses and the high cost of human life. The Battle of the Somme would have a lasting impact on the war and on the soldiers who fought in it, and it remains one of the most iconic and tragic battles of World War I.

High casualties and the toll on both sides

The Battle of the Somme was one of the bloodiest battles of World War I, resulting in staggering casualties on both sides. The scale of the human cost of the battle was immense, with hundreds of thousands of soldiers killed, wounded, or missing. The high casualties and the toll on both sides were a defining feature of the Battle of the Somme, shaping the course of the battle and its aftermath. Here's an overview of the high casualties and the toll on both sides:

British and Commonwealth Casualties:

The British and Commonwealth forces suffered heavy casualties during the Battle of the Somme. On the first day alone, July 1, 1916, the British Army suffered over 57,000 casualties, including nearly 20,000 dead.

By the end of the battle in November 1916, the British and Commonwealth forces had suffered over 400,000 casualties, including approximately 130,000 dead.

French Casualties:

The French forces also suffered heavy casualties during the Battle of the Somme, although their losses were not as severe as those of the British. The French suffered an estimated 200,000 casualties, including approximately 50,000 dead.

German Casualties:

The German Army also suffered significant casualties during the Battle of the Somme. Exact figures are difficult to determine, but it is estimated that the Germans suffered between 400,000 and 500,000 casualties, including approximately 160,000 dead.

The high casualties suffered by the Germans during the Battle of the Somme had a significant impact on their ability to continue fighting on the Western Front.

Human Cost:

The Battle of the Somme took a heavy toll on the soldiers who fought in it, both physically and mentally. Many soldiers suffered horrific injuries, including loss of limbs, disfigurement, and psychological trauma.

The high casualties and the brutal nature of the fighting at the Somme had a profound impact on the soldiers who survived, shaping their views of the war and its aftermath.

Legacy:

The Battle of the Somme left a lasting legacy of loss and suffering. It remains one of the most iconic and tragic battles of World War I, symbolizing the futility and horror of war.

The high casualties and the toll on both sides at the Battle of the Somme are a stark reminder of the human cost of war and the sacrifices made by the soldiers who fought in it.

Key Moments and Battles

The Battle of the Somme, fought from July to November 1916, consisted of several key moments and battles that shaped its outcome and its place in history. These key moments and battles were marked by intense fighting, strategic decisions, and significant losses on both sides. Here are some of the key moments and battles of the Battle of the Somme:

First Day, July 1, 1916:

The first day of the Battle of the Somme is remembered as one of the bloodiest days in British military history. The British Army suffered over 57,000 casualties, including nearly 20,000 killed.

Despite heavy losses, some British units managed to make limited gains, particularly in the south of the battlefield. However, these gains came at a high cost and did not lead to a breakthrough.

Capture of Mametz, July 7-11, 1916:

The capture of the village of Mametz was a key objective for the British during the early stages of the battle. The village was eventually captured by the British after several days of intense fighting.

The capture of Mametz was a significant achievement for the British, but it was only a small part of the larger battle and did not lead to a breakthrough.

Battle of Bazentin Ridge, July 14-17, 1916:

The Battle of Bazentin Ridge was one of the first major attacks by the British during the Battle of the Somme. The objective was to capture the German positions on Bazentin Ridge.

The British were successful in capturing the ridge after several days of heavy fighting. The capture of Bazentin Ridge gave the British a strategic advantage and allowed them to advance further into German-held territory.

Battle of Pozières, July 23-September 3, 1916:

The Battle of Pozières was another key moment in the Battle of the Somme. The village of Pozières was a key German strongpoint, and its capture was essential for the British advance.

The Battle of Pozières was marked by intense fighting and heavy casualties on both sides. The village was eventually captured by the British after several weeks of fighting.

Battle of Flers-Courcelette, September 15-22, 1916:

The Battle of Flers-Courcelette saw the first use of tanks in battle. The British used tanks to support their infantry assaults, with mixed results.

While the tanks were able to help break through some German defenses, many broke down or got stuck in the mud. Despite this, the British managed to make some gains during the battle.

End of the Battle, November 1916:

The Battle of the Somme officially ended in November 1916, as the onset of winter weather made further offensives difficult.

By the end of the battle, the British and French forces had advanced a few miles at most along a 15-mile front, at a cost of over a million casualties.

In conclusion, the Battle of the Somme was a complex and brutal battle, marked by several key moments and battles that shaped its outcome. Despite heavy casualties and limited gains, the Battle of the Somme remains one of the most iconic and tragic battles of World War I, symbolizing the futility and horror of war.

Battles for key objectives such as Mametz Wood and High Wood

The Battle of the Somme saw several key battles for important objectives, such as Mametz Wood and High Wood, which were pivotal in the overall campaign. These battles were marked by fierce fighting, heavy casualties, and strategic significance. Here's an overview of the battles for Mametz Wood and High Wood:

Battle of Mametz Wood, July 7-14, 1916:

Mametz Wood was a dense forest located near the village of Mametz, and its capture was a key objective for the British during the Battle of the Somme.

The battle for Mametz Wood began on July 7, 1916, and lasted for several days. The British forces faced stiff resistance from the German defenders, who were well-entrenched in the wood.

Despite heavy casualties, the British eventually managed to capture Mametz Wood by July 14, 1916. The battle was a costly victory, with both sides suffering significant losses.

Battle of High Wood, July 14-September 15, 1916:

High Wood was a strategically important position that overlooked the surrounding countryside, making it a key objective for both sides during the Battle of the Somme.

The battle for High Wood began on July 14, 1916, and lasted for several months. The wood changed hands several times during the course of the battle, as both sides launched multiple attacks and counterattacks.

The fighting in High Wood was characterized by close-quarters combat, with soldiers fighting among the trees and trenches. The wood was heavily fortified by both sides, making it difficult to capture and hold.

The British forces eventually captured High Wood on September 15, 1916, after a sustained and costly effort. The capture of High Wood was a significant achievement for the British, as it gave them a strategic advantage in the area.

The battles for Mametz Wood and High Wood were just two examples of the intense and costly fighting that took place during the Battle of the Somme. These battles, along with others fought during the campaign, highlighted the brutal nature of trench warfare and the high human cost of the war. The capture of key objectives such as Mametz Wood and High Wood was essential for the overall success of the Allied offensive on the Western Front, and their eventual capture played a significant role in shaping the outcome of the Battle of the Somme.

The struggle for control of the River Somme crossings

The Battle of the Somme, fought from July to November 1916, was a pivotal campaign of World War I that saw intense fighting for control of the River Somme crossings. The River Somme, flowing through the heart of the battlefield, served as a natural barrier that both sides sought to control to gain strategic advantage. The struggle for control of the River Somme crossings was a key aspect of the battle and played a crucial role in shaping its outcome. Here's an overview of the struggle for control of the River Somme crossings:

Strategic Importance of the River Somme:

The River Somme was a significant geographical feature that ran across the battlefield, dividing the Allied and German lines.

Controlling the River Somme crossings was crucial for both sides, as they provided key strategic points for launching offensives and defending against attacks.

Initial Situation:

At the start of the Battle of the Somme, the River Somme crossings were mostly in German hands. The Germans had fortified their positions along the river, making it difficult for the Allies to make significant advances.

Allied Offensives:

The Allies launched several offensives to capture the River Somme crossings and break through the German lines. These offensives were part of the broader strategy to push the Germans back and achieve a breakthrough on the Western Front.

The first major offensive to capture the River Somme crossings was the Battle of Albert, which began on July 1, 1916, with the British attack on the village of Fricourt and the French attack on the village of Curlu.

The Battle of Albert, July 1-13, 1916:

The Battle of Albert saw heavy fighting for control of the River Somme crossings, particularly at the towns of Albert and Peronne.

The British managed to capture the town of Albert on July 1, 1916, but progress was slow due to stiff German resistance and difficult terrain.

The French also made gains during the Battle of Albert, capturing several key positions along the river and pushing the Germans back.

The Battle of Bapaume, August 21-September 3, 1916:

The Battle of Bapaume saw further fighting for control of the River Somme crossings, particularly at the town of Bapaume.

The British and French forces launched a series of offensives to capture Bapaume and secure the river crossings. The town was eventually captured by the Allies on September 3, 1916, after heavy fighting.

The Battle of the Ancre Heights, October 1-November 11, 1916:

The Battle of the Ancre Heights was the final major offensive of the Battle of the Somme and saw further fighting for control of the River Somme crossings.

The British launched a series of attacks to capture the high ground overlooking the river and secure the crossings. The battle was marked by heavy casualties on both sides but resulted in significant gains for the Allies.

Outcome:

The struggle for control of the River Somme crossings was a key aspect of the Battle of the Somme and played a crucial role in shaping its outcome.

The Allies were ultimately successful in capturing the River Somme crossings and pushing the Germans back, although the cost in terms of human life was high.

In conclusion, the struggle for control of the River Somme crossings was a key aspect of the Battle of the Somme and played a crucial role in shaping its outcome. The Allies' success in capturing the river crossings was a significant achievement that helped pave the way for further advances on the Western Front.

The Aftermath

The aftermath of the Battle of the Somme, fought from July to November 1916, was characterized by profound consequences for both the Allied and German forces, as well as for the wider course of World War I. The battle resulted in staggering casualties, strategic realignments, and shifts in military tactics and technologies. Here's an overview of the aftermath of the Battle of the Somme:

Human Cost:

The Battle of the Somme was one of the bloodiest battles in history, resulting in over a million casualties on both sides. The British and French forces suffered over 600,000 casualties, including approximately 150,000 killed, while the German forces suffered similar losses.

The human cost of the battle was devastating, with entire units decimated and families torn apart. The scale of the casualties shocked the world and had a profound impact on the soldiers who fought in the battle.

Strategic Impact:

Despite the high casualties, the Battle of the Somme did not result in a decisive breakthrough for either side. The Allies made some territorial gains, but they fell far short of their initial objectives.

The battle did, however, have a strategic impact on the war. It forced the Germans to divert troops from other fronts to reinforce their positions on the Western Front, weakening their overall military strength.

Technological Developments:

The Battle of the Somme saw the introduction of new military technologies, such as tanks and improved artillery tactics.

While these technologies were not yet fully developed, they laid the groundwork for future advances in warfare.

Tactical Lessons:

The Battle of the Somme also provided valuable tactical lessons for both sides. The failure of large-scale infantry assaults led to a reevaluation of military tactics, with a greater emphasis placed on small-unit tactics and combined arms operations.

Political Consequences:

The Battle of the Somme had significant political consequences. In Britain, the high casualties and limited gains led to public outcry and calls for changes in military leadership.

In Germany, the battle reinforced the perception that the war was unwinnable, leading to growing discontent and unrest on the home front.

Legacy:

The Battle of the Somme left a lasting legacy on both sides. For the Allies, it was a symbol of courage and sacrifice, while for the Germans, it was a reminder of the horrors of war and the futility of further conflict.

The battle also had a profound impact on military strategy and tactics, influencing future military operations and shaping the course of World War I.

In conclusion, the aftermath of the Battle of the Somme was characterized by profound consequences for both the Allied and German forces, as well as for the wider course of World War I. The battle's staggering casualties, strategic realignments, and shifts in military tactics and technologies left a lasting impact on all those involved and played a crucial role in shaping the outcome of the war.

Assessment of the strategic outcome of the battle

The Battle of the Somme, fought from July to November 1916, was one of the largest and bloodiest battles of World War I. The strategic outcome of the battle has been the subject of much debate among historians, military analysts, and scholars. While the battle did not result in a decisive breakthrough or victory for either side, it had significant strategic implications for the course of the war. Here's an assessment of the strategic outcome of the Battle of the Somme:

Limited Tactical Success:

From a tactical perspective, the Battle of the Somme can be seen as a limited success for the Allies. They were able to capture significant amounts of territory from the Germans, including key positions along the front line.

However, these gains came at a high cost, with over a million casualties suffered by both sides. The high casualty rate and the failure to achieve a decisive breakthrough raised questions about the effectiveness of the Allied strategy.

Strategic Realignment:

The Battle of the Somme forced the Germans to divert troops from other fronts to reinforce their positions on the Western Front. This strategic realignment weakened the German military and contributed to their eventual defeat.

The battle also marked a turning point in the war, as it demonstrated the growing strength and capabilities of the Allied forces. The introduction of new military technologies,

141

such as tanks, further tilted the balance of power in favor of the Allies.

Psychological Impact:

The Battle of the Somme had a significant psychological impact on both sides. For the Allies, it was a symbol of their determination and sacrifice, while for the Germans, it was a sobering reminder of the costs of war.

The high casualty rate and the brutal nature of the fighting at the Somme served to demoralize both armies and their civilian populations, further eroding support for the war.

Long-Term Consequences:

The Battle of the Somme had long-term consequences for the course of the war. It set the stage for future offensives and campaigns on the Western Front, including the Allied Hundred Days Offensive in 1918 that ultimately led to the German surrender.

The battle also had a lasting impact on military strategy and tactics, influencing future operations and shaping the course of modern warfare.

In conclusion, while the Battle of the Somme did not result in a decisive victory for either side, it had significant strategic implications for the course of World War I. The battle's high casualty rate, strategic realignment, and psychological impact left a lasting legacy that is still felt to this day.

Impact on the British, French, and German forces

The Battle of the Somme, fought from July to November 1916, had a profound impact on the British, French, and German forces involved in the conflict. The battle was one of the largest and bloodiest of World War I, and its effects were felt by all sides. Here's an overview of the impact of the Battle of the Somme on the British, French, and German forces:

British Forces:

The Battle of the Somme had a significant impact on the British forces, both militarily and psychologically. The British Army suffered over 400,000 casualties, including approximately 130,000 killed, making it one of the costliest battles in British military history.

The battle also had a lasting impact on the British Army's tactics and strategy. The high casualty rate led to a reevaluation of military tactics, with a greater emphasis placed on small-unit tactics and combined arms operations.

Despite the heavy losses, the Battle of the Somme was seen as a symbol of British determination and sacrifice. It played a crucial role in shaping British identity and remembrance of the war.

French Forces:

The Battle of the Somme also had a significant impact on the French forces. The French Army suffered over 200,000 casualties, including approximately 50,000 killed, during the battle.

The battle highlighted the strength and resilience of the French Army, which played a crucial role in holding the line and preventing a German breakthrough.

The French forces also learned valuable lessons from the battle, particularly in the areas of artillery tactics and defensive warfare, which would prove useful in future battles.

German Forces:

The Battle of the Somme had a profound impact on the German forces. While the Germans were able to hold their ground and prevent a breakthrough, they suffered heavy casualties, with estimates ranging from 400,000 to 500,000 casualties, including approximately 160,000 killed.

The high casualty rate and the failure to achieve a decisive victory at the Somme had a demoralizing effect on the German forces. It also forced the Germans to divert troops from other fronts to reinforce their positions on the Western Front, weakening their overall military strength.

The Battle of the Somme also had a lasting impact on German military strategy and tactics. It highlighted the importance of defensive warfare and reinforced the Germans' determination to hold their ground at all costs.

In conclusion, the Battle of the Somme had a profound impact on the British, French, and German forces involved in the conflict. The battle's high casualty rate, strategic realignment, and psychological impact left a lasting legacy that is still felt to this day.

Legacy and Remembrance

The Battle of the Somme, fought from July to November 1916, left a lasting legacy that continues to be remembered and commemorated to this day. The battle, with its staggering casualties and brutal nature, has become a symbol of the futility and horror of war. Here's an overview of the legacy and remembrance of the Battle of the Somme:

Human Cost:

The Battle of the Somme resulted in over a million casualties, making it one of the bloodiest battles in history. The scale of the human cost of the battle shocked the world and left a profound impact on all those involved.

The high casualty rate and the brutal nature of the fighting at the Somme served as a stark reminder of the horrors of war and the sacrifices made by the soldiers who fought in it.

Military Lessons:

The Battle of the Somme also had a significant impact on military strategy and tactics. It highlighted the importance of careful planning, coordination, and innovation in military operations.

The introduction of new technologies, such as tanks and improved artillery tactics, further emphasized the need for military leaders to adapt to the changing nature of warfare.

Cultural Impact:

The Battle of the Somme had a profound cultural impact, influencing art, literature, and popular culture. Many poets and writers, such as Siegfried Sassoon and Wilfred Owen, drew inspiration from their experiences at the Somme.

The battle also had a lasting impact on remembrance and commemoration, with many memorials, monuments, and ceremonies dedicated to those who fought and died at the Somme.

Remembrance:

The Battle of the Somme is remembered and commemorated in various ways. In Britain and France, there are numerous memorials and cemeteries dedicated to the soldiers who fought and died at the Somme.

Anniversaries of the battle are also marked by ceremonies and events to honor the memory of those who served. The battle's legacy is kept alive through remembrance and education, ensuring that future generations understand the sacrifices made during the war.

Historical Significance:

The Battle of the Somme is seen as a turning point in World War I. While it did not result in a decisive victory for either side, it marked a shift in the balance of power on the Western Front.

The battle's legacy is one of resilience, sacrifice, and determination, as soldiers from both sides faced unimaginable hardships and challenges in the pursuit of their objectives.

In conclusion, the Battle of the Somme left a lasting legacy that continues to be remembered and commemorated. The battle's impact on military strategy, culture, and remembrance is a testament to the enduring significance of this historic event.

Commemoration of the battle and its significance in World War I history

The Battle of the Somme, fought from July to November 1916, is commemorated and remembered in various ways that highlight its significance in World War I history. The battle, with its enormous scale and devastating human cost, has become a symbol of the sacrifices made during the war and a focal point for remembrance and reflection. Here's an overview of the commemoration of the Battle of the Somme and its significance in World War I history:

Memorials and Cemeteries:

The Battle of the Somme is commemorated through numerous memorials and cemeteries dedicated to the soldiers who fought and died during the battle. These include the Thiepval Memorial to the Missing of the Somme, which bears the names of over 72,000 British and South African soldiers who have no known grave.

Other memorials, such as the Beaumont-Hamel Newfoundland Memorial, the Lochnagar Crater Memorial, and the Ulster Tower, also serve as reminders of the sacrifices made during the battle.

Remembrance Ceremonies:

Anniversaries of the Battle of the Somme are marked by remembrance ceremonies and events in Britain, France, and other countries involved in the conflict. These ceremonies often include wreath-laying ceremonies, moment of silence, and readings of poems and prayers.

The centenary of the Battle of the Somme in 2016 was marked by a series of events and commemorations in Britain and France, including a memorial service at the Thiepval Memorial attended by dignitaries and descendants of those who fought in the battle.

Educational Initiatives:

The Battle of the Somme is also commemorated through educational initiatives aimed at raising awareness about the history and significance of the battle. Museums, exhibitions, and educational programs provide insights into the experiences of those who fought in the battle and the impact it had on the course of the war.

These initiatives help to ensure that the memory of the Battle of the Somme is preserved for future generations and that the sacrifices made during the battle are not forgotten.

Symbol of Sacrifice:

The Battle of the Somme has become a symbol of the sacrifice and courage of the soldiers who fought in World War I. It is a reminder of the human cost of war and the need to strive for peace and reconciliation.

The commemorations of the Battle of the Somme serve as a poignant reminder of the impact of war on individuals, families, and communities, and the importance of remembering those who have served and sacrificed in conflicts around the world.

In conclusion, the Battle of the Somme is commemorated in various ways that highlight its significance in World War I history. Through memorials, ceremonies, and educational initiatives, the memory of the Battle of the Somme is preserved and its legacy is honored, ensuring that the sacrifices made during the battle are never forgotten.

Lessons learned from the Battle of the Somme

The Battle of the Somme, fought from July to November 1916, taught valuable lessons that influenced military strategy, tactics, and operations in the later years of World War I and beyond. Despite its high human cost and limited tactical success, the battle provided important insights that helped shape future military planning. Here are some key lessons learned from the Battle of the Somme:

Artillery Tactics:

The Battle of the Somme highlighted the importance of effective artillery tactics in supporting infantry assaults. The prolonged artillery bombardment before the infantry attack, though not as effective as hoped, demonstrated the need for improved coordination and timing between artillery and infantry units.

Infantry Tactics:

The Battle of the Somme showed the limitations of large-scale infantry assaults against well-fortified positions. It emphasized the need for more flexible and decentralized tactics, such as infiltration tactics, to avoid the heavy casualties suffered in frontal assaults.

Logistics and Supply:

The Battle of the Somme revealed the challenges of supplying and resupplying troops in a prolonged offensive. It underscored the importance of efficient logistics and supply lines to sustain military operations over extended periods.

Command and Control:

The Battle of the Somme exposed weaknesses in command and control structures, particularly in coordinating attacks between different units and nationalities. It highlighted the need for clearer communication and better coordination between allied forces.

Technology and Innovation:

The Battle of the Somme saw the introduction of new military technologies, such as tanks and improved artillery, which had a significant impact on future warfare. It demonstrated the potential of these technologies and the need for further development and integration into military operations.

Psychological and Moral Factors:

The Battle of the Somme highlighted the importance of morale and psychological factors in military operations. It showed that soldiers' morale could be severely affected by prolonged, costly battles, and that maintaining high morale was crucial for success.

Planning and Preparation:

The Battle of the Somme revealed the importance of thorough planning and preparation for military operations. It demonstrated that rushed, poorly planned offensives could lead to costly failures and unnecessary casualties.

Medical and Evacuation Practices:

The Battle of the Somme led to advancements in medical practices and evacuation procedures. It highlighted the need for better medical facilities and evacuation systems to care for wounded soldiers and prevent unnecessary deaths.

In conclusion, the Battle of the Somme was a costly and brutal battle that provided important lessons for military planners and strategists. The battle's impact on military tactics, technology, logistics, and command and control continues to be studied and analyzed, making it a crucial event in the history of modern warfare.

Gallipoli: The Failed Campaign

Introduction

The Gallipoli Campaign of World War I stands as a stark reminder of the horrors and futilities of war. What began as a bold strategic move by the Allied powers to secure a sea route to Russia and knock the Ottoman Empire out of the war quickly turned into a bloody and protracted stalemate. The campaign, which lasted from April 1915 to January 1916, resulted in immense human suffering, strategic miscalculations, and ultimately, a failure to achieve its objectives.

The Gallipoli Peninsula, located in modern-day Turkey, was the site of the ill-fated campaign. The Allies, led by Britain and France, aimed to capture the Dardanelles Strait, a narrow waterway that controlled access to the Black Sea and, by extension, Russia. The plan was to land troops on the peninsula, move inland, and then advance to capture Constantinople (modern-day Istanbul), the capital of the Ottoman Empire.

The campaign began on April 25, 1915, with a series of amphibious landings at Cape Helles and Anzac Cove. The landings were met with fierce resistance from the Ottoman defenders, who were well-entrenched and prepared for the assault. The rugged terrain of the peninsula, with its steep cliffs and narrow beaches, made progress slow and difficult for the Allies.

Despite initial gains and some tactical successes, the campaign soon bogged down into a stalemate. The Allies were unable to break through the Ottoman defenses, and the Ottomans, reinforced by German military advisors, proved to be formidable opponents. The fighting was brutal and unforgiving, with both sides suffering heavy casualties.

As the campaign dragged on, it became increasingly clear that the Allies' objectives were beyond reach. The harsh conditions, combined with the stubborn resistance of the Ottomans, made any further advances impossible. In January 1916, after months of bloody fighting and mounting casualties, the Allies finally decided to evacuate their remaining forces from the peninsula.

The Gallipoli Campaign was a costly failure for the Allies. The campaign resulted in over 100,000 Allied casualties, including over 44,000 dead. The Ottomans also suffered heavily, with estimates of their casualties ranging from 50,000 to 85,000. The campaign also had a significant impact on the course of the war, diverting resources and attention away from other theaters of operation.

The legacy of the Gallipoli Campaign is a complex and contentious one. For the Allies, it was a costly and humiliating defeat that exposed the limitations of their military strategy. For the Ottomans, it was a moment of triumph and a turning point in their struggle for independence. For the soldiers who fought and died on both sides, it was a tragic chapter in a war that would change the world forever.

In this book, we will explore the events leading up to the Gallipoli Campaign, the course of the campaign itself, and its aftermath. We will examine the strategic decisions, the military tactics, and the human stories that shaped this pivotal moment in history. Through the lens of Gallipoli, we will seek to understand the broader context of World War I and the impact it had on the lives of those who fought and died in its trenches.

The Strategic Importance of Gallipoli

The Gallipoli Campaign, launched by the Allied powers during World War I, was intended to secure a sea route to Russia and knock the Ottoman Empire out of the war. The campaign, however, ended in failure and became one of the most infamous episodes of the war. Despite its failure, Gallipoli held significant strategic importance for both the Allies and the Ottoman Empire. Here's an overview of the strategic importance of Gallipoli:

1.   Access to the Black Sea:

The primary objective of the Gallipoli Campaign was to secure a sea route to Russia through the Dardanelles Strait and the Black Sea. This would have allowed the Allies to supply Russia more easily and open up a new front against the Central Powers, particularly the Austro-Hungarian Empire.

2.   Knocking the Ottoman Empire out of the War:

The Ottoman Empire, allied with the Central Powers, controlled the Dardanelles and the Gallipoli Peninsula. Capturing these strategic points would have allowed the Allies to threaten Constantinople (Istanbul) and potentially force the Ottoman Empire to surrender or negotiate a separate peace.

3.   Strategic Diversion:

The Allies hoped that a successful campaign at Gallipoli would divert German and Austro-Hungarian forces away from the Eastern and Western Fronts, relieving pressure on the Allies in those theaters of war.

4.   Protecting British Interests:

The British Empire had significant interests in the Eastern Mediterranean and the Middle East, including access to oil reserves and the Suez Canal. Securing the Dardanelles would have protected these interests and ensured British control over key trade routes.

5.   Prestige and Morale:

The Gallipoli Campaign was seen as an opportunity to boost morale among the Allied forces and demonstrate their commitment to the war effort. A successful campaign would have been a significant propaganda victory for the Allies.

6.   Testing New Tactics and Technologies:

The Gallipoli Campaign saw the first large-scale use of amphibious warfare and the deployment of new military technologies, such as aircraft and submarines. The campaign provided valuable lessons in these areas, which would be applied in future conflicts.

Despite its strategic importance, the Gallipoli Campaign ended in failure for the Allies. The Ottoman defenses, combined with harsh terrain and logistical challenges, proved too formidable to overcome. The campaign resulted in heavy casualties on both sides and had a lasting impact on the course of the war.

In conclusion, while the Gallipoli Campaign ultimately failed to achieve its objectives, it remains a testament to the strategic significance of the Eastern Mediterranean and the complex interplay of politics, strategy, and military tactics during World War I. The legacy of Gallipoli continues to be remembered and studied as a pivotal moment in modern military history.

Dardanelles and its significance in World War I

The Dardanelles, a narrow strait in northwestern Turkey, connects the Aegean Sea to the Sea of Marmara and separates Europe from Asia. The strait is a vital waterway that has long been of strategic importance, serving as the gateway to the Black Sea. During World War I, the Dardanelles played a crucial role in the conflict, particularly in the Gallipoli Campaign. Here's an overview of the Dardanelles and its significance in World War I:

1. Strategic Location:

The Dardanelles served as a key strategic location due to its control over access to the Black Sea. Controlling the strait would allow naval forces to bypass the heavily fortified land defenses of the Ottoman Empire and access the Black Sea, providing a direct route to Russia.

2. Russian Access:

For the Allies, gaining control of the Dardanelles would provide a much-needed supply route to Russia, which was cut off from most of its traditional supply routes due to the Central Powers' control of the Baltic and Black Seas.

3. Ottoman Defenses:

The Ottoman Empire, aware of the strategic importance of the Dardanelles, had heavily fortified the strait with a series of forts, minefields, and coastal artillery batteries. These defenses made any attempt to force the strait a challenging and dangerous proposition.

4.   Naval Campaign:

In February 1915, the Allies launched a naval campaign to force the Dardanelles and capture Constantinople. The campaign, however, was met with strong resistance from the Ottoman defenders and failed to achieve its objectives.

5.   Gallipoli Campaign:

Following the failure of the naval campaign, the Allies launched a ground invasion of the Gallipoli Peninsula in April 1915, with the aim of securing the Dardanelles from land. The campaign, however, ended in failure and resulted in heavy casualties on both sides.

6.   Legacy:

The failure of the Gallipoli Campaign and the subsequent evacuation of Allied forces in January 1916 had far-reaching consequences. It led to the resignation of British First Lord of the Admiralty, Winston Churchill, and contributed to the downfall of the Asquith government in Britain.

The Gallipoli Campaign also had a lasting impact on the national consciousness of Australia and New Zealand, whose troops suffered heavy losses during the campaign. ANZAC Day, commemorated on April 25th each year, honors the memory of those who served and died at Gallipoli.

In conclusion, the Dardanelles and the Gallipoli Campaign were significant aspects of World War I, highlighting the strategic importance of control over key waterways and the challenges of modern warfare. The legacy of the Dardanelles and Gallipoli continues to be remembered and studied as a pivotal moment in military history.

Allied objectives and plans for the campaign

The Allied objectives and plans for the Gallipoli Campaign were ambitious but ultimately flawed, leading to one of the most infamous campaigns of World War I. The campaign, launched in April 1915, aimed to secure a sea route to Russia, knock the Ottoman Empire out of the war, and potentially open up a new front against the Central Powers. Here's an overview of the Allied objectives and plans for the Gallipoli Campaign:

1.   Secure a Sea Route to Russia:

One of the primary objectives of the Gallipoli Campaign was to secure a sea route to Russia through the Dardanelles Strait and the Black Sea. This would have allowed the Allies to supply Russia more easily and potentially open up a new front against the Central Powers.

2.   Knock the Ottoman Empire out of the War:

The Allies hoped that by capturing the Dardanelles and threatening Constantinople (Istanbul), the capital of the Ottoman Empire, they could force the Ottomans to surrender or negotiate a separate peace. This would have removed a key ally of the Central Powers from the war.

3.   Divert German and Austro-Hungarian Forces:

The Allies also hoped that a successful campaign at Gallipoli would divert German and Austro-Hungarian forces away from the Eastern and Western Fronts, relieving pressure on the Allies in those theaters of war.

4.   Capture Constantinople:

Capturing Constantinople was seen as a key objective of the campaign, as it would have opened up a direct route to the

Black Sea and potentially enabled the Allies to threaten the southern flank of the Central Powers.

5.   Initial Naval Assault:

The campaign began with a naval assault on the Dardanelles in February 1915, with the aim of forcing the strait and clearing the way for a larger amphibious landing.

6.   Amphibious Landings:

In April 1915, Allied forces landed troops at Cape Helles and Anzac Cove on the Gallipoli Peninsula. The landings were intended to secure a foothold on the peninsula and then advance inland to capture key objectives.

7.   Stalemate and Failure:

Despite initial gains and some tactical successes, the campaign quickly bogged down into a stalemate. The Allies were unable to break through the Ottoman defenses, and the Ottomans, reinforced by German military advisors, proved to be formidable opponents.

8.   Evacuation:

In January 1916, after months of bloody fighting and mounting casualties, the Allies decided to evacuate their remaining forces from the peninsula, bringing an end to the campaign.

In conclusion, the Allied objectives and plans for the Gallipoli Campaign were ambitious but ultimately flawed. The campaign's failure had far-reaching consequences and remains a poignant reminder of the challenges and horrors of modern warfare.

Planning and Preparations

Planning and preparations for the Gallipoli Campaign were extensive, involving detailed strategic, logistical, and operational considerations. The Allies, led by Britain and France, planned the campaign with the aim of securing a sea route to Russia and knocking the Ottoman Empire out of the war. Here's an overview of the planning and preparations for the battle:

1.   Strategic Planning:

The planning for the Gallipoli Campaign began in late 1914, with the Allies devising a strategy to capture the Dardanelles and open up a sea route to Russia. The campaign was part of a larger Allied strategy to break the stalemate on the Western Front and relieve pressure on the Eastern Front.

2.   Operational Planning:

The operational planning for the campaign involved detailed plans for the naval assault on the Dardanelles and the subsequent amphibious landings on the Gallipoli Peninsula. The plan called for a combined naval and land assault to secure key positions on the peninsula and advance inland.

3.   Logistical Preparations:

Logistical preparations for the campaign were extensive, involving the mobilization and deployment of troops, equipment, and supplies to the region. The Allies established supply depots and logistics bases to support the campaign and ensure the troops were adequately supplied.

4.   Intelligence Gathering:

Intelligence gathering played a crucial role in the planning and preparations for the campaign. The Allies conducted extensive reconnaissance and intelligence operations to gather information about Ottoman defenses, terrain, and troop movements.

5. Amphibious Assault Planning:

The amphibious assault on the Gallipoli Peninsula required careful planning and coordination. The Allies planned to land troops at multiple locations along the peninsula to secure a foothold and then advance inland to capture key objectives.

6. Naval Support:

The naval support for the campaign was provided by a combined Allied fleet, which included battleships, cruisers, and destroyers. The naval forces were tasked with bombarding Ottoman positions along the coast and providing support for the amphibious landings.

7. Tactical Preparations:

Tactical preparations for the campaign involved training troops in amphibious warfare and preparing them for the challenges of fighting in rugged terrain against a determined enemy. Troops were also briefed on the objectives and expected outcomes of the campaign.

8. Medical Preparations:

Medical preparations for the campaign included establishing field hospitals and medical facilities to care for the wounded. Medical personnel were trained in battlefield medicine and prepared to deal with the expected casualties of the campaign.

In conclusion, the planning and preparations for the Gallipoli Campaign were extensive and involved multiple aspects of military strategy and operations. Despite these preparations, the campaign ultimately ended in failure, highlighting the challenges and uncertainties of modern warfare.

Initial plans for the campaign?

The initial plans for the Gallipoli Campaign were ambitious and aimed at securing a sea route to Russia, knocking the Ottoman Empire out of the war, and potentially opening up a new front against the Central Powers. The campaign, launched in April 1915, began with a naval assault on the Dardanelles followed by amphibious landings on the Gallipoli Peninsula. Here's an overview of the initial plans for the campaign:

1.   Naval Assault on the Dardanelles:

The initial plan called for a naval assault on the Dardanelles Strait to force a passage through the Ottoman defenses and clear the way for a larger amphibious landing on the Gallipoli Peninsula.

2.   Amphibious Landings:

Following the successful naval assault, the plan called for Allied troops to land at multiple locations on the Gallipoli Peninsula to secure a foothold and then advance inland to capture key objectives, including high ground and strategic positions.

3.   Capture of Constantinople:

The ultimate objective of the campaign was to capture Constantinople (modern-day Istanbul), the capital of the Ottoman Empire. Capturing Constantinople would have opened up a direct route to the Black Sea and potentially enabled the Allies to threaten the southern flank of the Central Powers.

4.   Diversionary Attack:

As part of the initial plans, a diversionary attack was also launched at the Gulf of Saros to distract Ottoman forces and draw attention away from the main assault on the Dardanelles.

5.   Russian Support:

The Allies hoped that the campaign would receive support from Russian forces, who were fighting on the Eastern Front. A successful campaign at Gallipoli would have provided a much-needed supply route to Russia and relieved pressure on the Eastern Front.

6.   Limited Objectives:

Initially, the objectives of the campaign were limited to securing a sea route to Russia and threatening the Ottoman Empire. However, as the campaign progressed, the Allies hoped to achieve a more decisive victory by capturing Constantinople and knocking the Ottoman Empire out of the war.

In conclusion, the initial plans for the Gallipoli Campaign were bold and ambitious, aiming to achieve strategic objectives that would have had far-reaching consequences for the course of World War I. However, the campaign ultimately ended in failure, highlighting the challenges and uncertainties of modern warfare.

Troop deployments and naval operations

Troop deployments and naval operations played a crucial role in the Gallipoli Campaign, which aimed to secure a sea route to Russia and knock the Ottoman Empire out of World War I. The campaign, launched in April 1915, involved extensive troop deployments and naval operations by the Allied powers, primarily Britain and France. Here's an overview of troop deployments and naval operations during the Gallipoli Campaign:

1.   Troop Deployments:

The Allied forces assembled a multinational force for the Gallipoli Campaign, including troops from Britain, France, Australia, New Zealand, India, and other British Empire territories. The total number of troops deployed to Gallipoli varied but was estimated to be around 500,000.

2.   British Troops:

The British contingent was the largest, consisting of soldiers from various units of the British Army. They were deployed to different sectors of the Gallipoli Peninsula, including Cape Helles and Anzac Cove.

3.   ANZAC Troops:

The Australian and New Zealand Army Corps (ANZAC) played a significant role in the campaign, with troops landing at Anzac Cove on April 25, 1915. The ANZACs faced fierce resistance from Ottoman forces but managed to establish a foothold on the peninsula.

4.   French Troops:

French troops were also deployed to Gallipoli, primarily at the southern end of the peninsula near Cape Helles. The French forces supported the British and ANZAC troops in their efforts to advance inland.

5.   Naval Operations:

The Gallipoli Campaign began with a naval assault on the Dardanelles Strait in February 1915. The Allied naval forces, including battleships, cruisers, and destroyers, bombarded Ottoman positions along the coast and attempted to force a passage through the strait.

6.   Naval Bombardments:

The naval bombardments were intended to soften up Ottoman defenses and clear the way for the amphibious landings. However, the naval assault did not achieve its objectives, as Ottoman defenses proved to be more resilient than expected.

7.   Amphibious Landings:

The naval operations were followed by amphibious landings on the Gallipoli Peninsula in April 1915. Troops were landed at multiple locations, including Cape Helles and Anzac Cove, with the aim of securing a foothold and then advancing inland.

8.   Challenges and Setbacks:

The naval operations and troop deployments faced numerous challenges and setbacks, including rough seas, difficult terrain, and determined Ottoman resistance. Despite these challenges, the Allies managed to establish a foothold on the peninsula but were unable to achieve their objectives.

In conclusion, troop deployments and naval operations were critical aspects of the Gallipoli Campaign, which ultimately ended in failure for the Allies. The campaign highlighted the challenges of amphibious warfare and the complexities of modern military operations.

The Landings

The landings at Gallipoli on April 25, 1915, marked the beginning of one of the most significant and ill-fated campaigns of World War I. The Allied forces, primarily composed of troops from Britain, France, Australia, and New Zealand, launched a series of amphibious assaults on the Gallipoli Peninsula, with the aim of securing a sea route to Russia and knocking the Ottoman Empire out of the war. Here's an overview of the landings at Gallipoli:

GALLIPOLI: THE FAILED CAMPAIGN

1.   Objective and Strategy:

The objective of the landings was to establish a foothold on the Gallipoli Peninsula and then advance inland to capture key objectives, including high ground and strategic positions. The strategy was to secure a sea route to Russia and threaten Constantinople (modern-day Istanbul), the capital of the Ottoman Empire.

2.   Anzac Cove:

The Australian and New Zealand Army Corps (ANZAC) landed at Anzac Cove in the early hours of April 25, 1915. The landing was met with fierce resistance from Ottoman forces, and the ANZACs faced steep cliffs and rugged terrain as they attempted to advance inland.

3.   Cape Helles:

Simultaneously, British and French troops landed at Cape Helles, at the southern tip of the peninsula. The landing at Cape Helles was also met with strong resistance, and the troops struggled to establish a foothold on the shore.

4.   Challenges and Setbacks:

The landings at Gallipoli were plagued by a number of challenges and setbacks, including rough seas, difficult terrain, and determined Ottoman defenders. The rugged coastline made it difficult to land troops and supplies, and the Ottoman defenders had the advantage of high ground and well-fortified positions.

5.   Stalemate and Trench Warfare:

Despite initial gains and some tactical successes, the landings quickly bogged down into a stalemate. Both sides dug in and began a period of trench warfare, similar to the Western Front in France and Belgium.

6.   High Casualties:

The landings at Gallipoli resulted in heavy casualties on both sides. The ANZACs, in particular, suffered significant losses, with over 8,000 Australian and nearly 3,000 New Zealand soldiers killed during the campaign.

7.   Legacy:

The landings at Gallipoli had a lasting impact on the national consciousness of Australia and New Zealand, giving rise to the commemorative holiday of ANZAC Day, which honors the memory of those who served and died in the campaign.

In conclusion, the landings at Gallipoli were a bold but ultimately unsuccessful attempt by the Allies to achieve strategic objectives in World War I. The campaign highlighted the challenges and complexities of amphibious warfare and left a lasting legacy on the nations involved.

Overview of the amphibious assaults at Cape Helles, Anzac Cove, and Suvla Bay

The amphibious assaults at Cape Helles, Anzac Cove, and Suvla Bay were key components of the Gallipoli Campaign, launched by the Allies during World War I. These landings, which took place in April and August 1915, aimed to secure a sea route to Russia and knock the Ottoman Empire out of the war. Here's an overview of the amphibious assaults at Cape Helles, Anzac Cove, and Suvla Bay:

1.   Cape Helles:

Cape Helles, at the southern tip of the Gallipoli Peninsula, was the site of the main British and French landing on April 25, 1915. The landing at Cape Helles was intended to secure a foothold on the peninsula and then advance inland to capture key objectives, including high ground and strategic positions.

The landing at Cape Helles was met with strong resistance from Ottoman forces, and the troops struggled to establish a foothold on the shore. Despite initial gains, the British and French forces were unable to make significant progress inland, and the campaign quickly bogged down into a stalemate.

2.   Anzac Cove:

Anzac Cove, located north of Cape Helles, was the site of the Australian and New Zealand Army Corps (ANZAC) landing on April 25, 1915. The ANZACs faced steep cliffs and rugged terrain as they attempted to advance inland from the beach.

Like the landing at Cape Helles, the ANZAC landing at Anzac Cove was met with fierce resistance from Ottoman forces. Despite the difficult conditions, the ANZACs managed to establish a foothold on the peninsula and hold their position against Ottoman counterattacks.

3.   Suvla Bay:

Suvla Bay, located north of Anzac Cove, was the site of a second Allied landing in August 1915. The landing at Suvla Bay was intended to support the ANZACs at Anzac Cove and break the stalemate on the peninsula.

The landing at Suvla Bay was initially successful, with Allied forces securing a beachhead and advancing inland. However, the Allied commanders failed to exploit their early gains, and the campaign once again bogged down into a stalemate.

In conclusion, the amphibious assaults at Cape Helles, Anzac Cove, and Suvla Bay were key components of the Gallipoli Campaign. Despite initial successes, the campaign ultimately ended in failure for the Allies, highlighting the challenges and complexities of amphibious warfare. The campaign had a lasting impact on the nations involved and is remembered as one of the most significant and tragic episodes of World War I.

Challenges faced by the Allied forces during the landings

The Allied forces faced numerous challenges during the landings at Gallipoli, which contributed to the difficulties and ultimate failure of the campaign. These challenges ranged from difficult terrain and strong Ottoman defenses to inadequate planning and coordination. Here are some of the key challenges faced by the Allied forces during the landings:

1.   Difficult Terrain:

The rugged and hilly terrain of the Gallipoli Peninsula presented a significant challenge for the Allied forces. Steep cliffs, ravines, and gullies made it difficult to land troops and equipment, and hindered the movement of troops once they were ashore.

2.   Strong Ottoman Defenses:

The Ottoman Empire had heavily fortified the Gallipoli Peninsula, with a network of trenches, bunkers, and artillery positions. Ottoman forces were well-prepared and well-entrenched, making it difficult for the Allies to dislodge them.

3.   Lack of Surprise:

The element of surprise was lost during the Allied naval bombardment of the Dardanelles, which alerted the

Ottoman defenders to the impending landings. This allowed the Ottomans to prepare their defenses and reinforce key positions before the Allied troops arrived.

4.   Limited Intelligence:

The Allies had limited intelligence about the Ottoman defenses and terrain at Gallipoli, which hampered their planning and decision-making. This lack of information contributed to the difficulties faced by Allied troops during the landings.

5.   Inadequate Planning and Coordination:

The planning and coordination of the Gallipoli Campaign were flawed from the outset. The Allied forces were divided in their objectives and lacked a unified command structure, leading to confusion and inefficiency.

6.   Logistical Challenges:

The logistical challenges of supplying and supporting the Allied forces at Gallipoli were immense. The rugged terrain made it difficult to establish supply lines, and the lack of proper facilities and infrastructure hindered the resupply of troops.

7.   Weather and Climate:

The weather and climate at Gallipoli posed additional challenges for the Allied forces. The hot, dry summers and cold, wet winters took a toll on the troops, many of whom were ill-equipped for the harsh conditions.

8.   Determined Ottoman Resistance:

Perhaps the greatest challenge faced by the Allied forces was the determined resistance of the Ottoman defenders. Ottoman troops, reinforced by German military advisors, fought fiercely to defend their homeland, inflicting heavy casualties on the Allies.

In conclusion, the landings at Gallipoli were plagued by a multitude of challenges, which ultimately contributed to the failure of the campaign. Despite the bravery and determination of the Allied troops, the difficulties faced during the landings proved insurmountable, resulting in one of the most costly and ill-fated campaigns of World War I.

Stalemate and Suffering

The Gallipoli Campaign quickly descended into a stalemate, characterized by entrenched positions, brutal trench warfare, and immense suffering on both sides. The initial hopes of a swift victory and strategic breakthrough were dashed, and instead, the campaign became a protracted and bloody struggle. Here's an overview of the stalemate and suffering experienced during the Gallipoli Campaign:

Stalemate:

After the initial landings in April 1915, the campaign quickly bogged down into a stalemate. Both sides dug in along the rugged terrain of the Gallipoli Peninsula, establishing intricate networks of trenches, bunkers, and fortifications.

The rugged and hilly terrain, coupled with strong Ottoman defenses, made any significant advances by the Allies difficult. The frontlines remained largely static for much of the campaign, with neither side able to gain a decisive advantage.

Trench Warfare:

Trench warfare, similar to that on the Western Front, became the norm at Gallipoli. Troops on both sides endured the hardships of living and fighting in the trenches, which were often flooded, muddy, and infested with vermin.

The trenches were subjected to constant shelling and sniping, and soldiers on both sides lived under the constant threat of death or injury.

Casualties and Suffering:

The Gallipoli Campaign was marked by high casualties and immense suffering. The rugged terrain and strong defenses of the Ottomans made any advance by the Allies costly in terms of human life.

Both sides suffered heavy casualties during the campaign, with tens of thousands of soldiers killed, wounded, or missing in action. Diseases such as dysentery, typhoid, and malaria also took a heavy toll on the troops.

Supply Shortages:

The stalemate at Gallipoli was exacerbated by supply shortages and logistical difficulties. The rugged terrain and limited infrastructure made it difficult to supply and resupply the troops, leading to shortages of food, water, ammunition, and medical supplies.

Psychological Toll:

The stalemate and suffering at Gallipoli took a psychological toll on the troops. Many soldiers suffered from shell shock, a condition now known as post-traumatic stress disorder (PTSD), as a result of the constant shelling and the horrors of trench warfare.

Endurance and Resilience:

Despite the hardships and suffering, the soldiers at Gallipoli displayed remarkable endurance and resilience. They endured harsh conditions, facing not only the physical challenges of the campaign but also the mental and emotional strain of prolonged combat.

In conclusion, the stalemate and suffering experienced during the Gallipoli Campaign were emblematic of the larger tragedy of World War I. The campaign, which began with such high hopes, ended in failure and tragedy, leaving a lasting impact on the nations involved and the soldiers who fought and died on the shores of Gallipoli.

The establishment of the beachheads and the stalemate that followed

The establishment of the beachheads at Gallipoli was a crucial but challenging achievement for the Allied forces during the campaign. However, once the beachheads were established, the campaign quickly descended into a stalemate characterized by entrenched positions, fierce fighting, and heavy casualties. Here's an overview of the establishment of the beachheads and the stalemate that followed:

1.   Establishment of Beachheads:

The Allied forces landed at multiple locations along the Gallipoli Peninsula, including Cape Helles, Anzac Cove, and Suvla Bay, in April and August 1915. Despite facing strong Ottoman resistance, the Allies managed to establish beachheads at these locations and secure a foothold on the peninsula.

The establishment of the beachheads was a challenging and costly endeavor, with many soldiers losing their lives in the initial landings and subsequent fighting to secure the beachheads.

2. Trench Warfare and Stalemate:

Once the beachheads were established, the campaign quickly descended into a stalemate characterized by trench warfare. Both sides dug in along the rugged terrain of the peninsula, establishing intricate networks of trenches, bunkers, and fortifications.

The stalemate was exacerbated by the difficult terrain, strong Ottoman defenses, and limited mobility of troops. Despite several attempts to break the stalemate, neither side was able to gain a decisive advantage.

3. Fierce Fighting and Casualties:

The stalemate at Gallipoli was marked by fierce fighting and heavy casualties on both sides. Troops endured the hardships of living and fighting in the trenches, facing constant shelling, sniping, and the threat of disease.

The casualties at Gallipoli were staggering, with tens of thousands of soldiers killed, wounded, or missing in action. Diseases such as dysentery, typhoid, and malaria also took a heavy toll on the troops.

4. Supply Shortages and Logistics:

The stalemate was also exacerbated by supply shortages and logistical difficulties. The rugged terrain and limited infrastructure made it difficult to supply and resupply the troops, leading to shortages of food, water, ammunition, and medical supplies.

The supply shortages further hampered efforts to break the stalemate, as troops lacked the resources needed to sustain a prolonged offensive.

5. Psychological Toll:

The stalemate and the constant hardships of trench warfare took a psychological toll on the troops. Many soldiers suffered from shell shock, a condition now known as post-traumatic stress disorder (PTSD), as a result of the constant shelling and the horrors of war.

In conclusion, the establishment of the beachheads at Gallipoli was a significant achievement for the Allied forces, but it quickly led to a stalemate characterized by trench warfare, heavy casualties, and immense suffering. The campaign, which began with high hopes of a quick victory, ultimately ended in failure and tragedy, leaving a lasting impact on the nations involved and the soldiers who fought and died on the shores of Gallipoli.

Harsh conditions faced by soldiers on both sides

The soldiers on both sides of the Gallipoli Campaign faced harsh and grueling conditions, which added to the already immense challenges of warfare. The rugged terrain, extreme weather, lack of basic amenities, and constant threat of enemy fire made life on the Gallipoli Peninsula incredibly difficult for the troops. Here's an overview of the harsh conditions faced by soldiers on both sides:

1. Terrain:

The Gallipoli Peninsula's terrain was rugged and unforgiving, with steep cliffs, deep gullies, and rocky hillsides. Navigating this terrain was challenging for soldiers, especially when carrying heavy equipment and supplies.

2. Climate:

The climate on the Gallipoli Peninsula was harsh, with hot, dry summers and cold, wet winters. Soldiers had to endure extreme temperatures and weather conditions, which took a toll on their health and morale.

3.   Trench Warfare:

Trench warfare was a key feature of the Gallipoli Campaign, with soldiers on both sides living and fighting in trenches dug into the rocky soil. These trenches were often flooded, muddy, and infested with vermin, making them extremely unpleasant and unhealthy.

4.   Food and Water:

Soldiers on both sides faced shortages of food and water, especially during the summer months when temperatures soared. Rations were often meager and of poor quality, leading to malnutrition and illness among the troops.

5.   Disease:

Diseases such as dysentery, typhoid, and malaria were rampant on the Gallipoli Peninsula, due in part to the unsanitary conditions of the trenches and the lack of proper medical facilities. Many soldiers fell ill and died from these diseases.

6.   Constant Threat:

Soldiers on both sides lived under the constant threat of enemy fire, including artillery bombardments, sniper attacks, and infantry assaults. This constant threat added to the stress and anxiety of frontline life.

7.   Supply Shortages:

Supply shortages were a constant problem for soldiers on both sides, with shortages of ammunition, medical supplies, and other essentials. The difficult terrain and limited infrastructure made it difficult to supply and resupply the troops.

8. Psychological Toll:

The harsh conditions of life on the Gallipoli Peninsula took a psychological toll on the soldiers, many of whom suffered from shell shock (now known as post-traumatic stress disorder) as a result of the constant stress and trauma of war.

In conclusion, the soldiers on both sides of the Gallipoli Campaign faced incredibly harsh and challenging conditions, which added to the already immense challenges of warfare. Despite these hardships, the soldiers displayed remarkable resilience and courage in the face of adversity, enduring the horrors of war with dignity and bravery.

Leadership and Command

The leadership and command during the Gallipoli Campaign played a crucial role in shaping the course and outcome of the campaign. The Allied forces, primarily composed of British, French, Australian, and New Zealand troops, were led by a combination of experienced military commanders and political leaders. However, a series of strategic and tactical errors, coupled with poor decision-making and communication breakdowns, contributed to the ultimate failure of the campaign. Here's an overview of the leadership and command during the Gallipoli Campaign:

Allied Command Structure:

The Allied forces at Gallipoli were under the overall command of British General Sir Ian Hamilton, who was responsible for coordinating the efforts of the British, French, Australian, and New Zealand troops.

However, the Allied command structure was often disjointed and fragmented, with different national contingents operating semi-independently and pursuing their own objectives.

British Leadership:

General Sir Ian Hamilton was appointed as the commander of the Mediterranean Expeditionary Force (MEF), responsible for the Gallipoli Campaign. Hamilton was an experienced and respected commander but struggled with the complexities of the campaign.

Other British commanders, such as Major General Aylmer Hunter-Weston and Lieutenant General Sir William Birdwood, also played key roles in leading British and ANZAC forces during the campaign.

French Leadership:

The French forces at Gallipoli were under the command of General Henri Gouraud, who led the French Colonial Corps. The French forces primarily operated in the southern sector of the peninsula, near Cape Helles.

French leadership and coordination with the British forces were generally effective, although they faced similar challenges and setbacks as their British counterparts.

Australian and New Zealand Leadership:

The Australian and New Zealand troops, known as the ANZACs, were led by General Sir William Birdwood. Birdwood was highly regarded by his troops but faced difficulties in coordinating with other Allied forces.

ANZAC commanders, such as Major General Sir Alexander Godley and Major General William Bridges, also played important roles in leading their respective units.

Challenges and Errors:

The Gallipoli Campaign was marred by a series of strategic and tactical errors, many of which can be attributed to poor leadership and command decisions. These errors included inadequate planning and intelligence, underestimation of Ottoman defenses, and ineffective coordination between Allied forces.

The failure to achieve a decisive breakthrough and the subsequent stalemate can be partly attributed to these leadership and command failures.

Legacy:

The leadership and command during the Gallipoli Campaign have been the subject of much debate and scrutiny. While some commanders have been criticized for their decisions and actions, others have been praised for their leadership and bravery in the face of adversity.

The lessons learned from the leadership and command failures at Gallipoli have had a lasting impact on military strategy and doctrine, influencing future campaigns and operations.

In conclusion, the leadership and command during the Gallipoli Campaign were characterized by a mix of competence, bravery, and failure. While some leaders demonstrated skill and determination, others struggled to adapt to the challenges of the campaign, ultimately leading to its failure. The legacy of Gallipoli serves as a reminder of the importance of effective leadership and command in military operations.

Analysis of key leaders including Churchill, Hamilton, and Mustafa Kemal

The Gallipoli Campaign involved key leaders whose decisions and actions significantly influenced the course and outcome of the campaign. Among these leaders were Winston Churchill, who was First Lord of the Admiralty at the time and a key advocate for the campaign; Sir Ian Hamilton, the overall commander of the Allied forces; and Mustafa Kemal Atatürk, a young Ottoman officer who played a pivotal role in defending the Gallipoli Peninsula. Here's an analysis of these key leaders:

Winston Churchill:

As First Lord of the Admiralty, Churchill was a strong proponent of the Gallipoli Campaign, seeing it as a way to break the stalemate on the Western Front and open up a new front against the Central Powers.

Churchill's vision and enthusiasm for the campaign helped to push it forward, despite reservations from some military leaders. However, his strategic planning and decision-making have been criticized, particularly regarding the lack of adequate intelligence and underestimation of Ottoman defenses.

Churchill's reputation suffered as a result of the failure of the Gallipoli Campaign, and he was ultimately forced to resign from his position as First Lord of the Admiralty.

Sir Ian Hamilton:

Hamilton was appointed as the commander of the Mediterranean Expeditionary Force (MEF) and was responsible for planning and executing the Gallipoli Campaign.

Hamilton was an experienced and respected commander, but he struggled with the complexities of the campaign, including the difficult terrain, strong Ottoman defenses, and inadequate logistics.

Hamilton's leadership during the campaign has been criticized for a lack of clear strategic objectives, poor coordination between Allied forces, and failure to adapt to changing circumstances.

Mustafa Kemal Atatürk:

Mustafa Kemal Atatürk, then a young Ottoman officer, played a crucial role in the defense of the Gallipoli Peninsula. Atatürk's leadership and tactical skill were instrumental in repelling the Allied forces and preventing them from achieving their objectives.

Atatürk's actions at Gallipoli helped to establish his reputation as a military leader and statesman. He later became the founding father of the Republic of Turkey and is revered as a national hero.

Atatürk's leadership at Gallipoli is seen as a prime example of effective military leadership, characterized by strategic vision, tactical ingenuity, and the ability to inspire and motivate his troops.

In conclusion, the Gallipoli Campaign involved key leaders whose decisions and actions had a significant impact on the course and outcome of the campaign. Winston Churchill's advocacy for the campaign, Sir Ian Hamilton's command of the Allied forces, and Mustafa Kemal Atatürk's leadership in the defense of the Gallipoli Peninsula all played crucial roles in shaping the legacy of Gallipoli and the subsequent history of the nations involved.

Command decisions and their impact on the campaign

Command decisions during the Gallipoli Campaign played a critical role in shaping the course and outcome of the campaign. The decisions made by Allied commanders, including strategic planning, operational tactics, and logistical considerations, had a direct impact on the success or failure of the campaign. Here's an analysis of some key command decisions and their impact on the Gallipoli Campaign:

1.   Strategic Planning:

One of the key command decisions was the overall strategic planning for the campaign. The decision to launch a naval and amphibious assault on the Gallipoli Peninsula was based on the belief that it would lead to a quick victory and open up a new front against the Central Powers.

However, the strategic planning was flawed, with inadequate intelligence about Ottoman defenses and an underestimation of the difficulties of the terrain and logistics.

2.   Landing Sites:

The decision on where to land the Allied forces was crucial to the success of the campaign. The choice of multiple landing sites, including Cape Helles, Anzac Cove, and Suvla Bay, was intended to create multiple fronts and confuse the Ottoman defenders.

However, the decision to land at multiple sites also stretched Allied resources thin and made it difficult to concentrate their forces for a decisive breakthrough.

3.   Logistics and Resupply:

The command decisions regarding logistics and resupply were critical to sustaining the Allied forces on the Gallipoli

Peninsula. However, the difficult terrain and limited infrastructure made it challenging to establish and maintain supply lines.

The failure to adequately plan for logistics and resupply contributed to shortages of food, water, ammunition, and medical supplies, which hampered Allied operations.

4.   Tactical Maneuvers:

The command decisions regarding tactical maneuvers and engagements on the battlefield also had a significant impact on the campaign. The decision to launch costly frontal assaults against well-entrenched Ottoman positions resulted in heavy casualties for the Allies.

The failure to adapt to the realities of trench warfare and employ more innovative tactics contributed to the stalemate and ultimate failure of the campaign.

5.   Communication and Coordination:

Effective communication and coordination between Allied forces were crucial to the success of the campaign. However, the command decisions regarding communication and coordination were often lacking, leading to misunderstandings and missed opportunities.

The lack of a unified command structure and the semi-independent operations of different national contingents further hindered communication and coordination efforts.

In conclusion, the command decisions during the Gallipoli Campaign were critical in shaping the course and outcome of the campaign. Flawed strategic planning, inadequate logistics, ineffective tactical maneuvers, and poor communication and coordination all contributed to the failure of the campaign. The lessons learned from the command decisions at Gallipoli have had a lasting impact on military strategy and doctrine, influencing future campaigns and operations.

The August Offensive

The August Offensive, also known as the Battle of Sari Bair, was a major Allied offensive launched at Gallipoli in August 1915, with the aim of breaking the stalemate and capturing key objectives, including the high ground of Sari Bair and Chunuk Bair. The offensive was intended to be a decisive blow against the Ottoman defenses but ultimately ended in failure. Here's an overview of the August Offensive:

Objective and Planning:

The August Offensive was conceived as a bold plan to break the deadlock at Gallipoli by capturing the high ground overlooking the peninsula. The objectives included Hill 971 (Koja Chemen Tepe), Chunuk Bair, and Hill Q.

The offensive was part of a larger plan to link up the ANZAC and Suvla Bay beachheads and advance towards the vital high ground. The plan was ambitious but lacked adequate preparation and coordination.

Initial Successes:

The offensive began on the night of August 6, 1915, with a series of night attacks by ANZAC forces. Despite initial successes and the capture of some objectives, including the foothold on Chunuk Bair, the offensive soon stalled due to stiff Ottoman resistance and logistical difficulties.

Challenges and Setbacks:

The August Offensive faced a number of challenges and setbacks, including difficult terrain, strong Ottoman defenses, and inadequate artillery and supplies. The Allied forces also suffered from poor communication and coordination, which hindered their ability to consolidate their gains.

The lack of a clear plan for exploitation and reinforcement meant that the initial gains made by the ANZAC forces were not adequately supported, allowing the Ottomans to launch counterattacks and retake lost ground.

Stalemate and Failure:

Despite several days of fierce fighting, the August Offensive failed to achieve its objectives. The Allied forces were unable to secure the high ground of Sari Bair and Chunuk Bair, and the offensive ultimately devolved into a stalemate, with both sides digging in and entrenching their positions.

The failure of the August Offensive marked the end of any hopes for a quick victory at Gallipoli and highlighted the challenges and difficulties faced by the Allied forces in overcoming the Ottoman defenses.

Legacy:

The August Offensive is remembered as a bold but ultimately failed attempt to break the stalemate at Gallipoli. The offensive highlighted the difficulties of waging war in the harsh terrain of the Gallipoli Peninsula and the challenges of coordinating large-scale offensives.

The lessons learned from the August Offensive, including the importance of adequate preparation, coordination, and logistics, would later influence Allied strategy in other theaters of the war.

In conclusion, the August Offensive was a significant but unsuccessful attempt by the Allies to break the stalemate at Gallipoli. Despite initial successes, the offensive was hampered by a lack of preparation, coordination, and adequate support, ultimately leading to its failure and the continuation of the stalemate on the Gallipoli Peninsula.

Overview of the Allied attempt to break the stalemate

The Allied attempt to break the stalemate at Gallipoli was a series of offensives and operations aimed at securing key objectives and ultimately defeating the Ottoman forces. The Allies, primarily composed of British, French, Australian, and New Zealand troops, launched several major offensives, including the August Offensive, in an effort to achieve a breakthrough. However, these attempts were met with stiff resistance, logistical challenges, and ultimately ended in failure. Here's an overview of the Allied attempt to break the stalemate at Gallipoli:

1.   Strategic Objectives:

The Allies' primary objective was to secure the Dardanelles Strait and open up a supply route to Russia, which would alleviate pressure on the Eastern Front and potentially knock the Ottoman Empire out of the war.

To achieve this, the Allies planned a series of naval and amphibious assaults on the Gallipoli Peninsula, with the ultimate goal of capturing Constantinople (modern-day Istanbul) and forcing the Ottoman Empire to surrender.

2.   Naval Campaign:

The Allied naval campaign, launched in February 1915, aimed to force the Dardanelles and allow Allied ships to sail through to the Sea of Marmara. However, the naval campaign failed to achieve its objectives, as Ottoman defenses proved too strong.

3.   Amphibious Landings:

In April 1915, the Allies launched a series of amphibious landings at multiple locations along the Gallipoli Peninsula, including Cape Helles, Anzac Cove, and Suvla Bay.

The landings were intended to secure beachheads and allow Allied forces to advance inland, but they were met with fierce Ottoman resistance and bogged down into a stalemate.

4.   Offensives and Operations:

Throughout the campaign, the Allies launched several offensives and operations in an attempt to break the stalemate and achieve a decisive victory. These included the August Offensive, the Battle of Sari Bair, and the Battle of Krithia.

Despite initial successes and some gains, these offensives ultimately failed to achieve their objectives due to a combination of factors, including strong Ottoman defenses, difficult terrain, and inadequate planning and coordination.

5.   Stalemate and Evacuation:

By late 1915, it became clear that the Allies were unable to achieve a breakthrough at Gallipoli. The campaign had devolved into a stalemate, with both sides entrenched and unable to make significant advances.

In December 1915 and January 1916, the Allies began a gradual evacuation of their forces from Gallipoli, with the last troops leaving the peninsula in January 1916.

In conclusion, the Allied attempt to break the stalemate at Gallipoli was a series of ambitious but ultimately unsuccessful offensives and operations. Despite their efforts, the Allies were unable to achieve their strategic objectives and were forced to evacuate their forces from the peninsula. The campaign highlighted the challenges of waging war in difficult terrain and the importance of adequate planning, coordination, and logistics in military operations.

Battles for key objectives such as Lone Pine and Chunuk Bair

The Battles for key objectives such as Lone Pine and Chunuk Bair were critical engagements during the Gallipoli Campaign, representing some of the fiercest fighting and heroic actions on both sides. These battles were part of larger offensives and operations aimed at capturing key strategic positions and breaking the stalemate on the Gallipoli Peninsula. Here's an overview of the Battles for Lone Pine and Chunuk Bair:

1.   Battle of Lone Pine:

The Battle of Lone Pine took place between August 6 and August 10, 1915, during the broader August Offensive. The objective of the battle was to capture a series of Turkish trenches at Lone Pine, a strategically important position.

The battle began with a massive artillery bombardment followed by a coordinated infantry assault. Australian forces, primarily from the 1st Australian Division, led the attack and managed to capture the Turkish trenches after fierce hand-to-hand combat.

The battle was marked by intense fighting, with both sides suffering heavy casualties. The Australians, in particular, displayed remarkable bravery and determination in the face of stiff resistance.

2.   Battle of Chunuk Bair:

The Battle of Chunuk Bair, also known as the Battle of Hill Q, was a key engagement during the August Offensive. The objective of the battle was to capture the high ground of

Chunuk Bair, which overlooked the ANZAC positions and offered a strategic vantage point.

The battle began on August 6, 1915, with an assault by New Zealand forces from the Wellington Battalion. The New Zealanders managed to capture Chunuk Bair but were soon surrounded by Turkish forces and subjected to fierce counterattacks.

Despite several attempts to reinforce and resupply the New Zealanders, they were eventually forced to withdraw from Chunuk Bair due to heavy casualties and lack of support. The battle was a costly failure for the Allies and marked a turning point in the August Offensive.

3.   Significance:

The Battles for Lone Pine and Chunuk Bair were significant for their intensity and the high casualties suffered by both sides. These battles highlighted the difficulties of the terrain and the tenacity of the Turkish defenders.

The battles also showcased the bravery and determination of the ANZAC forces, who fought valiantly against overwhelming odds. Despite the ultimate failure to hold Chunuk Bair, the battles became symbols of ANZAC courage and sacrifice.

In conclusion, the Battles for Lone Pine and Chunuk Bair were critical engagements during the Gallipoli Campaign, representing some of the fiercest fighting and heroic actions of the campaign. These battles are remembered for the bravery and sacrifice of the soldiers involved and their significance in the broader narrative of the Gallipoli Campaign.

Evacuation and Aftermath

The evacuation of Allied forces from Gallipoli and its aftermath marked the end of one of the most infamous campaigns of World War I. The evacuation was a complex and risky operation that was carried out under the cover of darkness and with meticulous planning to avoid detection by Ottoman forces. Here's an overview of the evacuation and its aftermath:

Planning and Preparation:

The decision to evacuate the Allied forces from Gallipoli was made in late 1915, as it became clear that the campaign was untenable and that further efforts to break the stalemate would likely result in heavy casualties.

Planning for the evacuation began in November 1915, with preparations made to ensure that troops, equipment, and supplies could be safely withdrawn from the peninsula.

Execution of the Evacuation:

The evacuation was carried out in two stages, with the first phase involving the withdrawal of troops from the Suvla Bay and ANZAC Cove sectors in December 1915. This phase was largely successful, with the majority of troops evacuated without major incident.

The second phase, involving the withdrawal from the Cape Helles sector, took place in January 1916. This phase was more challenging, as Ottoman forces were more alert to the possibility of an evacuation and launched several attacks in an attempt to disrupt the withdrawal.

Despite these challenges, the evacuation was largely successful, with the last Allied troops leaving Gallipoli on January 9, 1916. The evacuation was a remarkable feat of military planning and execution, with minimal casualties suffered by the withdrawing forces.

Aftermath:

The evacuation of Gallipoli marked the end of a campaign that had cost the lives of hundreds of thousands of soldiers from both sides. The campaign had failed to achieve its objectives and had instead resulted in a costly stalemate that lasted for months.

The evacuation had a profound impact on the nations involved, particularly Australia and New Zealand, where the campaign had a significant impact on national identity and memory. The ANZAC legend, which emerged from the Gallipoli Campaign, remains a central part of Australian and New Zealand identity to this day.

The evacuation also had broader implications for the course of World War I, as it freed up Allied forces for other theaters of the war and allowed for a reevaluation of strategy and tactics.

In conclusion, the evacuation of Allied forces from Gallipoli marked the end of a campaign that had become a symbol of the futility and horror of war. The evacuation was a remarkable achievement and had a lasting impact on the nations involved and the course of World War I.

Decision to evacuate the troops from Gallipoli

The decision to evacuate the troops from Gallipoli was a culmination of several factors that made the continuation of the campaign untenable. By late 1915, it was clear to Allied commanders that the objectives of the Gallipoli Campaign were unlikely to be achieved, and further efforts would result in unnecessary casualties. Here's an overview of the factors that led to the decision to evacuate:

1. Stalemate and Casualties:

The Gallipoli Campaign had been ongoing for several months by late 1915, and despite several major offensives, the Allied forces had failed to achieve a decisive breakthrough. The campaign had devolved into a costly stalemate, with both sides suffering heavy casualties.

2. Logistical Challenges:

The harsh terrain and limited infrastructure of the Gallipoli Peninsula presented significant logistical challenges for the Allied forces. Supply lines were long and vulnerable to Ottoman attacks, making it difficult to adequately support and sustain the troops.

Health and Morale:

The harsh conditions of Gallipoli, including the extreme heat, poor sanitation, and constant threat of disease, had taken a toll on the health and morale of the troops. Many soldiers were suffering from illnesses such as dysentery and malaria, further reducing their effectiveness.

3. Strategic Realignment:

By late 1915, the strategic situation of World War I had shifted, with Allied priorities shifting to other theaters of the war, particularly the Western Front. The continuation of the Gallipoli Campaign was seen as a diversion of resources from more pressing fronts.

4. Enemy Strength:

Ottoman forces had proven to be more resilient and determined than expected, and their defenses had proved difficult to overcome. The Ottoman army had been reinforced, making any further attempts to break the stalemate increasingly risky.

5.   Military Advice:

Military commanders, including General Sir Ian Hamilton, the overall commander of the Allied forces at Gallipoli, had recommended the evacuation of the troops as the best course of action. They believed that further efforts to break the stalemate would only result in more casualties without achieving any significant gains.

In conclusion, the decision to evacuate the troops from Gallipoli was a pragmatic one, based on a realistic assessment of the situation on the ground and the strategic priorities of the Allied forces. The evacuation was ultimately carried out successfully, with minimal casualties, and marked the end of a campaign that had become a symbol of the futility and tragedy of war.

Assessment of the campaign's impact on the war effort

The Gallipoli Campaign, while ultimately a failure in achieving its objectives, had a significant impact on the broader war effort and the course of World War I. The campaign, which lasted from April 1915 to January 1916, involved a series of naval and amphibious operations by the Allies aimed at securing the Dardanelles Strait and opening up a supply route to Russia. Here's an assessment of the campaign's impact on the war effort:

1.   Diversion of Resources:

One of the key impacts of the Gallipoli Campaign was its diversion of resources from other theaters of the war. The campaign tied down a significant number of Allied troops and resources, which could have been used elsewhere, particularly on the Western Front.

2.   Loss of Lives:

The Gallipoli Campaign resulted in heavy casualties for both sides, with estimates of up to 250,000 casualties, including over 130,000 deaths. The campaign was particularly costly for the Allies, with a significant number of Australian, New Zealand, British, and French troops losing their lives.

3.   Impact on National Identity:

The Gallipoli Campaign had a profound impact on the national identity of Australia and New Zealand, where it is remembered as a symbol of sacrifice and endurance. The ANZAC legend, which emerged from the campaign, remains a central part of Australian and New Zealand identity.

4.   Strategic Implications:

The failure of the Gallipoli Campaign had strategic implications for the Allies, as it deprived them of a potential supply route to Russia and failed to knock the Ottoman Empire out of the war. The campaign also had a negative impact on Allied morale and reputation.

5.   Tactical Innovation:

Despite its ultimate failure, the Gallipoli Campaign did see some tactical innovations, particularly in the use of amphibious warfare and the development of new tactics and strategies for assaulting fortified positions.

6.   Impact on Ottoman Empire:

While the Gallipoli Campaign was a costly endeavor for the Allies, it also had significant consequences for the Ottoman Empire. The successful defense of Gallipoli boosted Ottoman morale and demonstrated the empire's ability to withstand Allied offensives.

In conclusion, the Gallipoli Campaign had a significant impact on the war effort, with far-reaching consequences for both the Allies and the Ottoman Empire. While it failed to achieve its immediate objectives, the campaign had lasting effects on the nations involved and the course of World War I.

Legacy and Lessons Learned

The Gallipoli Campaign left a profound legacy that has shaped the national identities of the nations involved and influenced military thinking and strategy. The campaign, which lasted from April 1915 to January 1916, resulted in heavy casualties and ultimately ended in failure for the Allies. However, the legacy of Gallipoli extends far beyond its military outcome. Here are some key aspects of the legacy of the Gallipoli Campaign:

National Identity:

The Gallipoli Campaign had a profound impact on the national identities of Australia and New Zealand, where it is remembered as a symbol of sacrifice, endurance, and mateship. The ANZAC legend, which emerged from the campaign, remains a central part of Australian and New Zealand identity.

Commemoration and Remembrance:

The Gallipoli Campaign is commemorated annually on ANZAC Day, April 25th, in Australia and New Zealand, as a day of remembrance for those who served and died in all wars, conflicts, and peacekeeping operations. The day is marked by dawn services, marches, and ceremonies.

Military Strategy:

The Gallipoli Campaign had a significant impact on military thinking and strategy, particularly in the areas of amphibious warfare, logistics, and planning. The campaign highlighted the challenges of conducting operations in difficult terrain and reinforced the importance of thorough planning and coordination.

Lessons Learned:

The Gallipoli Campaign taught valuable lessons about the importance of intelligence, planning, and coordination in military operations. It also highlighted the need for flexibility and adaptability in the face of changing circumstances and the importance of understanding the terrain and the enemy's capabilities.

Impact on World War I:

While the Gallipoli Campaign failed to achieve its immediate objectives, it had broader implications for World War I. The campaign tied down significant Allied resources and had a negative impact on Allied morale and reputation. It also boosted Ottoman morale and demonstrated the empire's ability to withstand Allied offensives.

International Relations:

The Gallipoli Campaign had lasting effects on international relations, particularly in the Middle East. The failure of the campaign contributed to the eventual dissolution of the Ottoman Empire and the redrawing of the map of the region.

In conclusion, the Gallipoli Campaign left a lasting legacy that continues to be felt today. It is remembered as a symbol of sacrifice and endurance, and its lessons have had a profound impact on military strategy and national identity.

The campaign serves as a reminder of the human cost of war and the importance of remembrance.

Commemoration of the campaign and its significance in Australian, New Zealand, British, and Turkish history

The commemoration of the Gallipoli Campaign holds significant importance in the histories of Australia, New Zealand, Britain, and Turkey, shaping national identities and influencing cultural traditions. The campaign, fought from April 1915 to January 1916, resulted in profound impacts on these nations and is remembered annually through various ceremonies and memorials. Here's a look at the commemoration of the campaign and its significance in each country's history:

Australia and New Zealand:

ANZAC Day, observed on April 25th each year, commemorates the landing of Australian and New Zealand troops (the ANZACs) at Gallipoli in 1915. It is a day to remember all Australians and New Zealanders who served and died in wars, conflicts, and peacekeeping operations.

ANZAC Day is marked by dawn services, marches, and ceremonies across Australia and New Zealand, as well as in locations around the world where Australian and New Zealand troops have served.

The Gallipoli Campaign is a central part of the national identity of Australia and New Zealand, symbolizing courage, sacrifice, and mateship.

Britain:

The Gallipoli Campaign is remembered in Britain as a significant chapter in the nation's military history. British troops played a major role in the campaign, alongside troops from Australia, New Zealand, and other Allied nations.

While the campaign ended in failure for the Allies, it is commemorated as a testament to the bravery and sacrifice of those who served.

Turkey:

In Turkey, the Gallipoli Campaign is remembered as a great victory that helped to defend the nation against foreign invasion. The campaign is seen as a turning point in Turkey's struggle for independence and is commemorated as a national holiday known as Çanakkale Victory and Martyrs' Day.

The Gallipoli Peninsula is home to numerous memorials and cemeteries, both Allied and Turkish, that serve as a reminder of the cost of war and the importance of peace.

In conclusion, the commemoration of the Gallipoli Campaign is a significant part of the histories of Australia, New Zealand, Britain, and Turkey. It serves as a reminder of the sacrifices made by those who served and died in the campaign and has helped to shape national identities and cultural traditions in these countries.

Lessons learned from the failed campaign for future military operations

The Gallipoli Campaign, while ultimately a failure for the Allies, provided valuable lessons that have informed military operations and strategy in the years since. The campaign, fought from April 1915 to January 1916, highlighted the importance of careful planning, coordination, and adaptability in military operations. Here are some key lessons learned from the failed campaign for future military operations:

1. Amphibious Warfare:

The Gallipoli Campaign demonstrated the challenges of conducting amphibious operations, particularly in hostile terrain and against determined defenders. The campaign underscored the need for thorough planning, intelligence, and coordination in such operations.

2. Logistics and Supply:

The campaign highlighted the critical importance of logistics and supply lines in sustaining military operations. The difficult terrain and harsh conditions of Gallipoli made it challenging to maintain adequate supplies for the troops, emphasizing the need for robust logistical planning.

3. Terrain and Environment:

The rugged terrain and harsh environment of Gallipoli posed significant challenges for the Allied forces, impacting their ability to maneuver and sustain operations. The campaign underscored the importance of understanding and adapting to the terrain and environment in military planning.

4. Intelligence and Reconnaissance:

The Gallipoli Campaign revealed the limitations of Allied intelligence and reconnaissance efforts, leading to insufficient information about Ottoman defenses and terrain. The campaign emphasized the need for accurate and timely intelligence in military planning.

5. Command and Leadership:

The campaign raised questions about command and leadership, particularly regarding the effectiveness of Allied leadership and decision-making. The failure of the campaign highlighted the importance of strong, decisive leadership in military operations.

6.   Adaptability and Flexibility:

The Gallipoli Campaign demonstrated the importance of adaptability and flexibility in military operations. The Allies struggled to adapt to changing circumstances and were unable to overcome the challenges posed by the Ottoman defenses.

7.   Lessons in Defeat:

While the Gallipoli Campaign ended in defeat for the Allies, it provided valuable lessons that shaped future military operations. The campaign highlighted the importance of learning from failure and applying those lessons to future endeavors.

In conclusion, the Gallipoli Campaign provided important lessons in military planning, logistics, intelligence, command, and adaptability. While it was a costly failure for the Allies, the campaign has had a lasting impact on military thinking and strategy, influencing future operations and shaping the course of military history.

Clash of Titans: The Battle of Jutland

Introduction

"Clash of Titans: The Battle of Jutland" was a pivotal naval engagement fought during World War I between the British Royal Navy's Grand Fleet and the Imperial German Navy's High Seas Fleet. The battle, which took place on May 31 to June 1, 1916, in the North Sea near the coast of Denmark's Jutland Peninsula, was the largest naval battle of the war and one of the most significant in naval history. Here's an overview of the Battle of Jutland:

Background:

By 1916, the British Royal Navy had imposed a blockade on Germany, leading the Germans to seek a decisive naval engagement to break the blockade and challenge British naval superiority.

The German High Seas Fleet, under the command of Admiral Reinhard Scheer, sought to lure out and destroy elements of the British Grand Fleet, commanded by Admiral Sir John Jellicoe.

Forces and Strategies:

The British Grand Fleet consisted of 28 battleships and 9 battlecruisers, while the German High Seas Fleet comprised 16 battleships and 5 battlecruisers.

The British strategy was to engage the German fleet in a decisive battle, while the Germans aimed to inflict maximum damage and then retreat to port safely.

The Battle:

The battle began on the afternoon of May 31, 1916, when British and German scouting forces made contact off the coast of Jutland.

Over the next several hours, the two fleets engaged in a series of engagements, with both sides suffering significant losses.

The battle continued into the early hours of June 1, with both fleets maneuvering for advantage and attempting to inflict damage on the enemy.

Outcome:

The Battle of Jutland was a tactical victory for the Germans, who inflicted greater losses on the British fleet in terms of ships and personnel.

However, the British retained control of the North Sea and maintained their blockade of Germany, preventing the High Seas Fleet from achieving its strategic objectives.

Significance:

The Battle of Jutland was the largest and most significant naval battle of World War I, involving over 250 ships and around 100,000 men.

The battle demonstrated the limitations of naval power in the modern era, with both sides failing to achieve a decisive victory.

The battle also highlighted the importance of tactics, technology, and strategy in naval warfare, influencing future developments in naval doctrine and design.

In conclusion, the Battle of Jutland was a pivotal moment in naval history, showcasing the challenges and complexities of modern naval warfare. The battle's legacy continues to be studied by naval historians and has had a lasting impact on naval strategy and tactics.

Naval Arms Race and Tensions

The Naval Arms Race and tensions leading up to World War I were characterized by a competition between the major European powers, particularly Britain and Germany, to build up their naval forces. This race for naval supremacy had far-reaching consequences and contributed to the growing tensions in Europe that ultimately led to the outbreak of World War I. Here's an overview of the Naval Arms Race and tensions:

Background:

In the late 19th and early 20th centuries, Britain had the world's most powerful navy, with its fleet serving as the backbone of its global empire.

Germany, a rising power seeking to expand its influence, began to challenge Britain's naval supremacy by building up its own fleet.

Naval Build-Up:

The Naval Arms Race began in the 1890s and intensified in the early 20th century, as both Britain and Germany sought to outbuild each other in terms of battleships and cruisers.

Other powers, such as France, Russia, and the United States, also expanded their navies in response to the growing tensions and perceived threats.

Technological Advancements:

The Naval Arms Race spurred advancements in naval technology, including the development of larger, more powerful battleships armed with heavy guns.

The introduction of the dreadnought battleship by Britain in 1906 revolutionized naval warfare and further escalated the arms race.

Political Tensions:

The Naval Arms Race exacerbated political tensions between Britain and Germany, as well as other European powers.

The growing naval build-up was seen as a threat to the balance of power in Europe and contributed to a sense of mistrust and rivalry between nations.

Diplomatic Efforts:

Efforts were made to control the naval arms race through diplomatic means, such as the 1908-09 London Naval Conference, which aimed to limit the size and growth of naval fleets.

However, these efforts were largely unsuccessful, and the naval build-up continued unabated.

Impact on World War I:

The Naval Arms Race and tensions it created were a contributing factor to the outbreak of World War I in 1914.

The naval build-up had created a volatile and unstable situation in Europe, with the major powers on edge and ready to mobilize their forces at a moment's notice.

In conclusion, the Naval Arms Race and tensions leading up to World War I were a reflection of the geopolitical rivalries and power struggles of the time. The competition for naval supremacy helped to set the stage for the outbreak of war and had a lasting impact on the course of 20th-century history.

Overview of the naval buildup and tensions between Britain and Germany

The naval buildup and tensions between Britain and Germany in the late 19th and early 20th centuries were a key aspect of the Naval Arms Race that contributed to the outbreak of World War I. The rivalry between the two powers was driven by a combination of strategic, political, and economic factors, leading to a significant buildup of naval forces on both sides. Here's an overview of the naval buildup and tensions between Britain and Germany:

1.   Strategic Considerations:

Britain, as an island nation with a vast empire, relied heavily on its navy to protect its overseas interests and maintain control of key sea routes.

Germany, a rapidly industrializing power seeking to expand its influence, viewed a strong navy as essential for securing its own economic and strategic interests, particularly its growing overseas colonies.

2.   Naval Expansion:

The Naval Arms Race between Britain and Germany began in the 1890s and intensified in the early 20th century, with both powers seeking to outbuild each other in terms of battleships, cruisers, and other naval vessels.

Germany's decision to build a powerful fleet, including the introduction of the dreadnought battleship in 1906, challenged Britain's traditional naval supremacy and sparked fears of a potential threat to British interests.

3. Political and Economic Factors:

The naval buildup was driven not only by military considerations but also by political and economic factors. Both Britain and Germany saw their naval strength as a reflection of their national prestige and power.

The naval buildup also had significant economic implications, as it spurred industrial production and technological innovation in both countries.

4. Tensions and Diplomatic Efforts:

The naval buildup and the rivalry between Britain and Germany contributed to a sense of tension and mistrust between the two powers.

Efforts were made to control the naval arms race through diplomatic means, including the 1908-09 London Naval Conference, but these efforts were largely unsuccessful in halting the buildup of naval forces.

5. Impact on World War I:

The naval buildup and tensions between Britain and Germany were a contributing factor to the outbreak of World War I in 1914.

The rivalry between the two powers helped to create a volatile and unstable situation in Europe, with the major powers on edge and ready to mobilize their forces in response to any perceived threat.

In conclusion, the naval buildup and tensions between Britain and Germany were a significant factor in the lead-up to World War I, highlighting the role of naval power in shaping global politics and the dynamics of international relations in the early 20th century.

Strategic importance of the North Sea in World War I

The North Sea played a crucial strategic role in World War I, serving as a major theatre of naval warfare and a key battleground between the Allied and Central Powers. The North Sea was strategically important for several reasons:

1.   Naval Blockade:

The North Sea was vital for enforcing the British naval blockade of Germany, which aimed to cut off essential supplies and resources from reaching the Central Powers.

The blockade had a significant impact on Germany's ability to sustain its war effort, contributing to food shortages and economic hardship.

2.   Control of Sea Lanes:

Control of the North Sea allowed for the protection of vital sea lanes and trade routes, ensuring the safe passage of supplies, troops, and reinforcements for the Allies.

The North Sea was also a key route for the transport of troops and supplies between Britain and continental Europe.

3.   Protection of British Isles:

The North Sea served as a defensive barrier for the British Isles, protecting them from potential naval attacks by the German High Seas Fleet.

British control of the North Sea helped to safeguard the British mainland and maintain the security of the British Empire.

4.   Naval Engagements:

The North Sea was the scene of several major naval engagements, including the Battle of Jutland in 1916, the largest naval battle of World War I.

These battles were fought for control of the sea and had a significant impact on the course of the war and the balance of power in the region.

5.   Submarine Warfare:

The North Sea was a key area for submarine warfare, with both sides deploying submarines to attack enemy shipping and disrupt supply lines.

The use of submarines, particularly by Germany with its U-boat campaign, had a major impact on the war at sea and on civilian shipping.

6.   Air Operations:

The North Sea was also important for air operations, with both sides using aircraft for reconnaissance, bombing raids, and anti-submarine warfare.

The development of naval aviation during World War I further increased the strategic importance of the North Sea.

In conclusion, the North Sea was of critical strategic importance in World War I, serving as a vital theater of naval warfare and a key battleground between the Allied and Central Powers. Control of the North Sea was crucial for enforcing blockades, protecting sea lanes, and securing the British Isles, making it a focal point of military operations and strategic planning during the war.

Prelude to Battle of Jutland

The Battle of Jutland, fought from May 31 to June 1, 1916, was the largest naval battle of World War I and one of the most significant engagements in naval history. The battle took place in the North Sea, near the coast of Denmark's Jutland Peninsula, between the British Grand Fleet, under

Admiral Sir John Jellicoe, and the German High Seas Fleet, under Admiral Reinhard Scheer. Here's a detailed overview of the Prelude to the Battle of Jutland:

Naval Buildup:

In the years leading up to World War I, Britain and Germany engaged in a naval arms race, building up their fleets in a competition for naval supremacy.

By 1916, the British Grand Fleet and the German High Seas Fleet were the two most powerful naval forces in the world, with both sides seeking a decisive naval engagement.

Strategic Objectives:

The British Grand Fleet sought to maintain control of the North Sea and protect Britain's maritime interests, including its vital sea lanes and trade routes.

The German High Seas Fleet aimed to challenge British naval supremacy and disrupt the British blockade of Germany, which was severely impacting the German war effort.

German Plans:

The German plan for the Battle of Jutland, known as Operation "Mikado," called for a diversionary raid on the British coast to draw out elements of the British Grand Fleet, which would then be engaged and defeated by the main German fleet.

Admiral Scheer hoped to achieve a decisive victory over the British fleet and break the British blockade, allowing German naval forces greater freedom of movement.

British Preparations:

The British Grand Fleet, based at Scapa Flow in the Orkney Islands, was alerted to the German fleet's movements through intelligence reports and intercepted communications.

Admiral Jellicoe ordered the Grand Fleet to sortie from its base to intercept the German fleet and prevent it from achieving its objectives.

Opening Moves:

The Battle of Jutland began on the afternoon of May 31, 1916, as the British and German fleets made contact in the North Sea.

The initial engagements were inconclusive, with both sides maneuvering for advantage and attempting to gain the upper hand in the battle.

Tactical Developments:

The battle saw the first major engagement between fleets of modern battleships and battlecruisers, highlighting the importance of speed, firepower, and armor in naval warfare.

Both sides suffered significant losses, with several ships sunk or heavily damaged in the course of the battle.

Aftermath:

The Battle of Jutland ended inconclusively, with neither side achieving a decisive victory.

The British Grand Fleet maintained control of the North Sea, but the German High Seas Fleet avoided a decisive defeat and was able to return to port relatively intact.

In conclusion, the Prelude to the Battle of Jutland was characterized by the buildup of naval forces, strategic planning, and preparations for what would become the largest naval battle of World War I. The battle marked a significant moment in naval history, showcasing the challenges and complexities of modern naval warfare.

Naval strategies and preparations of the British Grand Fleet and the German High Seas Fleet

The naval strategies and preparations of the British Grand Fleet and the German High Seas Fleet during World War I were shaped by their respective goals, capabilities, and the strategic imperatives of the conflict. Here's an overview of their strategies and preparations:

British Grand Fleet:

1.   Strategy:

The primary strategy of the British Grand Fleet, under the command of Admiral Sir John Jellicoe, was to maintain control of the North Sea and protect Britain's maritime interests.

The fleet's main objectives were to blockade Germany, protect merchant shipping, and prevent the German High Seas Fleet from gaining control of the sea.

2.   Preparations:

The British Grand Fleet was based at Scapa Flow in the Orkney Islands, a strategically important location that provided protection and easy access to the North Sea.

The fleet consisted of battleships, battlecruisers, cruisers, and destroyers, and it was supported by a network of bases and naval installations around the British Isles.

3.   Tactics:

The British Grand Fleet adopted a defensive strategy, avoiding decisive engagements unless the odds were heavily in their favor.

The fleet relied on its numerical superiority and superior firepower to deter and defeat the German High Seas Fleet in battle.

German High Seas Fleet:

1.   Strategy:

The primary strategy of the German High Seas Fleet, under the command of Admiral Reinhard Scheer, was to challenge British naval supremacy and disrupt the British blockade.

The fleet's goal was to engage and defeat the British Grand Fleet in a decisive battle, either in the North Sea or in a surprise raid on British coastal targets.

2.   Preparations:

The German High Seas Fleet was based at Wilhelmshaven and Kiel, with access to the North Sea and the Baltic Sea.

The fleet consisted of battleships, battlecruisers, cruisers, and submarines, and it was supported by a network of coastal defenses and naval bases.

3.   Tactics:

The German High Seas Fleet adopted an aggressive strategy, seeking opportunities to engage the British Grand Fleet in battle while avoiding being drawn into a decisive engagement.

The fleet also relied on its submarines, known as U-boats, to disrupt British shipping and naval operations.

In conclusion, the naval strategies and preparations of the British Grand Fleet and the German High Seas Fleet during World War I were shaped by their respective goals and capabilities. The British Grand Fleet focused on maintaining control of the North Sea and protecting Britain's maritime interests, while the German High Seas Fleet sought to challenge British naval supremacy and disrupt the British blockade. These strategies influenced their tactics and preparations for naval warfare, shaping the course of the naval conflict in World War I.

Intelligence and reconnaissance efforts leading up to the battle

Intelligence and reconnaissance efforts played a crucial role in the lead-up to the Battle of Jutland, providing commanders with vital information about enemy movements, strengths, and intentions. Both the British Grand Fleet and the German High Seas Fleet relied on a variety of intelligence-gathering methods to gather information and gain a strategic advantage. Here's an overview of the intelligence and reconnaissance efforts leading up to the Battle of Jutland:

1.   Aerial Reconnaissance:

Both sides used aircraft for reconnaissance, employing reconnaissance planes to gather information about enemy positions, troop movements, and fleet deployments.

Aerial reconnaissance provided valuable intelligence but was limited by the technology of the time and the dangers of flying over enemy territory.

2.   Naval Reconnaissance:

Both fleets deployed scouting forces, including cruisers and destroyers, to gather information about enemy fleet movements and positions.

These reconnaissance missions were often risky and required skilled and experienced sailors to gather accurate information.

3.   Signal Intelligence:

Both sides intercepted and deciphered enemy communications to gather intelligence about enemy intentions and operations.

Signal intelligence, or SIGINT, provided valuable information but was limited by the need to decrypt enemy codes and the risk of enemy interception.

4.   Agent Networks:

Both sides operated networks of spies and agents behind enemy lines, gathering information about enemy fleet movements, deployments, and intentions.

These agent networks were often risky and relied on skilled operatives to gather accurate and timely information.

5.   Reconnaissance by Fire:

Both sides used long-range naval gunfire to probe enemy positions and gather intelligence about enemy defenses and fleet deployments.

This method, known as "reconnaissance by fire," was a crude but effective way to gather intelligence about enemy positions.

6.   Scouting and Observation:

Both fleets used scouting forces, including cruisers and destroyers, to gather information about enemy fleet movements and positions.

Observation posts, manned by trained observers, were also used to gather information about enemy fleet movements and positions.

In conclusion, intelligence and reconnaissance efforts were critical in the lead-up to the Battle of Jutland, providing commanders with vital information that shaped their strategies and tactics. Despite the limitations of the technology of the time, both sides made significant efforts to gather intelligence and gain a strategic advantage in the battle.

The Battle Begins

The Battle of Jutland, fought from May 31 to June 1, 1916, was the largest naval battle of World War I and one of the most significant engagements in naval history. The battle took place in the North Sea, near the coast of Denmark's Jutland Peninsula, between the British Grand Fleet, under Admiral Sir John Jellicoe, and the German High Seas Fleet, under Admiral Reinhard Scheer. Here's an overview of the Battle of Jutland's commencement:

Initial Contact:

The battle began on the afternoon of May 31, 1916, as the British and German fleets made contact in the North Sea.

The British fleet, which had been alerted to the presence of the German fleet through intercepted communications and reconnaissance efforts, was prepared for battle.

1.   Opening Engagements:

The initial engagements were inconclusive, with both sides maneuvering for advantage and attempting to gain the upper hand in the battle.

The British and German fleets exchanged long-range gunfire, with both sides scoring hits on enemy ships but failing to achieve a decisive advantage.

2. German Maneuver:

Admiral Scheer, commanding the German High Seas Fleet, sought to draw the British fleet into a decisive engagement, hoping to achieve a significant victory and break the British blockade.

Scheer ordered his fleet to engage the British fleet aggressively, using a combination of battleships, battlecruisers, and other vessels to press the attack.

3. British Response:

Admiral Jellicoe, commanding the British Grand Fleet, adopted a cautious approach, seeking to preserve his fleet's numerical advantage and avoid a decisive engagement unless conditions were favorable.

Jellicoe ordered his fleet to maintain a defensive formation, using his battleships and battlecruisers to engage the German fleet at long range.

4. Tactical Developments:

The Battle of Jutland saw the first major engagement between fleets of modern battleships and battlecruisers, highlighting the importance of speed, firepower, and armor in naval warfare.

Both sides suffered significant losses, with several ships sunk or heavily damaged in the course of the battle.

5. Night Actions:

As darkness fell on May 31, the battle continued into the night, with both sides maneuvering to gain advantage in the darkness.

The night actions saw further engagements between the British and German fleets, but the darkness limited the effectiveness of both sides' gunfire.

In conclusion, the commencement of the Battle of Jutland was characterized by initial engagements, maneuvering for advantage, and the exchange of long-range gunfire. The battle would continue into the night and the following day, ultimately resulting in significant losses for both sides and shaping the course of naval warfare in World War I.

Initial contact between British and German naval forces

The initial contact between British and German naval forces during the Battle of Jutland took place on the afternoon of May 31, 1916, in the North Sea near the coast of Denmark's Jutland Peninsula. The encounter marked the beginning of one of the largest and most significant naval battles of World War I. Here's an overview of the initial contact between British and German naval forces:

1.   British Grand Fleet's Awareness:

The British Grand Fleet, under the command of Admiral Sir John Jellicoe, was alerted to the presence of the German High Seas Fleet through intercepted communications and reconnaissance efforts.

British naval intelligence had been monitoring German fleet movements and was prepared for a possible encounter with the German fleet.

2.   German High Seas Fleet's Movements:

The German High Seas Fleet, under the command of Admiral Reinhard Scheer, had set out from its bases in Wilhelmshaven and Kiel with the intention of engaging the British fleet.

Scheer had formulated a plan to draw out elements of the British Grand Fleet and engage them in a decisive battle.

3. Initial Reconnaissance:

Both sides deployed scouting forces, including cruisers and destroyers, to gather information about enemy fleet movements and positions.

These scouting forces played a crucial role in providing early warning of the enemy's presence and determining the location of the opposing fleet.

4. First Sighting:

The first sighting of the enemy fleet occurred when British and German scouting forces made visual contact with each other.

The sighting prompted both sides to prepare for battle, with the British fleet moving to intercept the German fleet and the German fleet preparing to engage the British.

5. Opening Engagements:

The initial engagements between British and German forces were characterized by long-range gunfire, as both sides attempted to score hits on enemy ships.

The British and German fleets exchanged fire as they maneuvered for advantage, with both sides seeking to gain the upper hand in the battle.

6. Continuation of the Battle:

The initial contact between British and German forces marked the beginning of a larger engagement that would continue into the night and the following day.

The Battle of Jutland would see further engagements between the two fleets, resulting in significant losses on both sides and shaping the course of naval warfare in World War I.

In conclusion, the initial contact between British and German naval forces during the Battle of Jutland set the stage for a larger and more decisive engagement between the two fleets. The encounter highlighted the challenges and complexities of naval warfare and set the tone for the rest of the battle.

Maneuvering and initial engagements

After the initial contact between British and German naval forces at the Battle of Jutland, both sides began maneuvering to gain a tactical advantage and engage the enemy fleet. The maneuvering and initial engagements were crucial in shaping the course of the battle and determining the outcome. Here's an overview of the maneuvering and initial engagements during the Battle of Jutland:

1.   Maneuvering for Position:

Both the British Grand Fleet and the German High Seas Fleet maneuvered to gain a favorable position relative to the enemy.

The fleets attempted to cross each other's "T," a tactical maneuver that would allow them to bring more guns to bear on the enemy while minimizing their own exposure.

2.   Initial Engagements:

The initial engagements between British and German forces were characterized by long-range gunfire, as both sides attempted to score hits on enemy ships.

The British and German fleets exchanged fire as they maneuvered for position, with both sides seeking to gain the upper hand in the battle.

3. British Battlecruiser Action:

One of the most significant early actions of the battle was the engagement between British and German battlecruisers.

The British battlecruisers, under the command of Admiral David Beatty, engaged the German battlecruisers, resulting in the loss of several ships on both sides.

4. German Fleet's Turn Away:

As the battle progressed, Admiral Scheer, commanding the German High Seas Fleet, ordered a turn away from the British fleet to avoid a decisive engagement.

The maneuver was intended to draw the British fleet closer to the German main fleet, where it could be engaged more effectively.

5. British Fleet's Pursuit:

The British Grand Fleet, under the command of Admiral Jellicoe, pursued the retreating German fleet, seeking to bring it to battle.

The pursuit continued into the night and the following day, as the British fleet sought to engage the German fleet and achieve a decisive victory.

In conclusion, the maneuvering and initial engagements during the Battle of Jutland were crucial in shaping the course of the battle and determining the outcome. The early actions of the battle set the stage for a larger and more decisive engagement between the two fleets, resulting in significant losses on both sides and shaping the course of naval warfare in World War I.

The Main Action

The main action of the Battle of Jutland took place on the afternoon and evening of May 31, 1916, as the British Grand Fleet and the German High Seas Fleet engaged in a fierce naval battle in the North Sea. The main action was characterized by intense gunfire, maneuvering for position, and tactical decisions that would ultimately shape the outcome of the battle. Here's an overview of the main action of the Battle of Jutland:

Initial Engagements:

The main action began with both fleets exchanging long-range gunfire, as they maneuvered to gain a tactical advantage.

The British and German fleets sought to bring their heaviest guns to bear on the enemy while minimizing their own exposure to enemy fire.

British Battlecruiser Losses:

One of the key moments of the main action was the loss of several British battlecruisers, including HMS Indefatigable, HMS Queen Mary, and HMS Invincible.

These losses were a result of the British battlecruisers' thinner armor compared to their German counterparts, which made them vulnerable to enemy fire.

German Battle Line:

As the main action progressed, the German High Seas Fleet formed a battle line, with the intention of engaging the British Grand Fleet at close range.

The German battle line was designed to maximize the firepower of the fleet's battleships and cruisers against the British fleet.

British Grand Fleet's Response:

In response to the German battle line formation, Admiral Jellicoe, commanding the British Grand Fleet, ordered his fleet to adopt a defensive formation.

The British fleet sought to maintain a safe distance from the German fleet while continuing to engage with long-range gunfire.

Night Actions:

As darkness fell, the main action continued into the night, with both fleets maneuvering and engaging in sporadic gunfire.

The darkness limited visibility and made it difficult for the fleets to maintain contact with each other, leading to confusion and uncertainty on both sides.

End of the Main Action:

The main action of the Battle of Jutland ended inconclusively, with neither side achieving a decisive victory.

Both fleets suffered significant losses, but the British Grand Fleet maintained control of the North Sea, preventing the German High Seas Fleet from achieving its objectives.

In conclusion, the main action of the Battle of Jutland was a fierce and intense naval battle that shaped the course of naval warfare in World War I. The engagement highlighted the challenges and complexities of modern naval warfare and resulted in significant losses on both sides.

The clash of the battlecruisers at the start of the battle

The clash of the battlecruisers at the start of the Battle of Jutland was a pivotal moment in the engagement, showcasing both the strengths and weaknesses of these formidable warships. The British and German battlecruiser squadrons, led by Admiral David Beatty and Admiral Franz von Hipper respectively, played a significant role in the early stages of the battle. Here's an overview of the clash of the battlecruisers at the start of the battle:

1.   British Battlecruiser Squadron:

Admiral Beatty's battlecruiser squadron, consisting of ships like HMS Lion, HMS Princess Royal, and HMS Indomitable, led the British advance.

Beatty intended to draw out the German fleet and engage them in a decisive battle, using the superior speed and firepower of his battlecruisers.

2.   German Battlecruiser Squadron:

Admiral Hipper's battlecruiser squadron, including ships like SMS Lützow, SMS Derfflinger, and SMS Seydlitz, prepared to engage the British forces.

Hipper sought to lure the British battlecruisers into range of the main German fleet, where they could be surrounded and overwhelmed.

3.   Initial Encounter:

The two battlecruiser squadrons made contact in the early afternoon of May 31, 1916, as British and German forces spotted each other's ships.

The British battlecruisers opened fire at long range, targeting the German vessels and attempting to disable them with accurate gunfire.

4.   British Losses:

The early stages of the clash saw significant losses for the British battlecruisers, with ships like HMS Indefatigable, HMS Queen Mary, and HMS Invincible being sunk.

These losses highlighted the vulnerability of the British battlecruisers, which had been designed for speed and firepower but lacked adequate armor protection.

5.   German Response:

The German battlecruisers responded to the British fire, targeting the British vessels with their own heavy guns and attempting to inflict maximum damage.

The German ships, with their thicker armor and powerful guns, were better able to withstand the British fire and inflict serious damage on the British battlecruisers.

6.   Outcome:

The clash of the battlecruisers at the start of the Battle of Jutland set the stage for a larger and more decisive engagement between the British Grand Fleet and the German High Seas Fleet.

While the British suffered significant losses in their battlecruiser squadron, the engagement helped to shape the tactics and strategy of the rest of the battle.

In conclusion, the clash of the battlecruisers at the start of the Battle of Jutland was a key moment in the engagement, highlighting the strengths and weaknesses of these powerful warships. The engagement set the stage for the larger naval battle that would follow, ultimately shaping the course of naval warfare in World War I.

The "Run to the South" and the main fleet engagements

The "Run to the South" refers to a critical phase during the Battle of Jutland on May 31, 1916, where the British and German fleets disengaged and repositioned themselves for a larger fleet engagement. This phase followed the initial clashes of the battlecruisers and preceded the main fleet

KEY CAMPAIGNS OF WORLD WAR I

engagements. Here's an overview of the "Run to the South" and the main fleet engagements that followed:

1.   Disengagement of the Battlecruisers:

After the initial clash of the battlecruisers, both Admiral Beatty's British battlecruiser squadron and Admiral Hipper's German battlecruiser squadron disengaged and maneuvered to the south.

The disengagement was prompted by the heavy losses suffered by both sides and the need to regroup and reassess the situation.

2.   Repositioning of the Fleets:

Following the disengagement of the battlecruisers, both the British Grand Fleet, under Admiral Jellicoe, and the German High Seas Fleet, under Admiral Scheer, repositioned their fleets for a larger engagement.

The British fleet moved to the northeast, while the German fleet moved to the southeast, with both sides preparing to engage in a decisive battle.

3.   Main Fleet Engagements:

The main fleet engagements began later in the evening of May 31, as the British and German fleets came into contact once again.

The engagement was characterized by intense gunfire and maneuvering, as both sides sought to gain the upper hand in the battle.

4.   British Grand Fleet's Strategy:

Admiral Jellicoe, commanding the British Grand Fleet, adopted a cautious approach, seeking to preserve his fleet's numerical advantage and avoid a decisive engagement unless conditions were favorable.

Jellicoe ordered his fleet to maintain a defensive formation, using his battleships and battlecruisers to engage the German fleet at long range.

5. German High Seas Fleet's Strategy:

Admiral Scheer, commanding the German High Seas Fleet, sought to draw the British fleet into a decisive engagement, hoping to achieve a significant victory and break the British blockade.

Scheer ordered his fleet to engage the British fleet aggressively, using a combination of battleships, battlecruisers, and other vessels to press the attack.

6. Outcome of the Main Fleet Engagements:

The main fleet engagements of the Battle of Jutland ended inconclusively, with neither side achieving a decisive victory.

Both fleets suffered significant losses, but the British Grand Fleet maintained control of the North Sea, preventing the German High Seas Fleet from achieving its objectives.

In conclusion, the "Run to the South" and the main fleet engagements were critical phases of the Battle of Jutland, shaping the course of the battle and determining its outcome. The engagements highlighted the challenges and complexities of naval warfare in World War I and resulted in significant losses on both sides.

Key Moments and Decisions

The Battle of Jutland, fought from May 31 to June 1, 1916, during World War I, was a pivotal naval engagement between the British Grand Fleet and the German High Seas

Fleet. Several key moments and decisions during the battle influenced its outcome and the course of naval warfare. Here are some of the key moments and decisions:

Deployment of the Battlecruisers:

The deployment of the British and German battlecruiser squadrons, under Admirals Beatty and Hipper respectively, set the stage for the initial clashes of the battle.

The decision to use these fast, heavily armed ships to scout and engage the enemy fleet proved critical in shaping the early stages of the battle.

Initial Clashes:

The initial clashes between the British and German battlecruisers, resulting in the loss of several ships on both sides, highlighted the vulnerability of these vessels to enemy fire.

These early engagements set the tone for the rest of the battle and influenced the strategies adopted by both fleets.

Run to the South:

The "Run to the South" phase of the battle, following the initial clashes, saw both fleets disengage and reposition for a larger engagement.

This phase allowed both sides to regroup and prepare for the main fleet engagements that would follow.

Main Fleet Engagements:

The main fleet engagements, characterized by intense gunfire and maneuvering, were the most critical phase of the battle.

Key decisions regarding tactics, positioning, and firepower during these engagements influenced the outcome of the battle.

British Grand Fleet's Strategy:

Admiral Jellicoe's cautious strategy, seeking to preserve the British fleet's numerical advantage and avoid a decisive engagement unless conditions were favorable, shaped the course of the battle.

Jellicoe's decision to maintain a defensive formation and engage the German fleet at long range played a crucial role in the battle's outcome.

German High Seas Fleet's Strategy:

Admiral Scheer's aggressive strategy, seeking to draw the British fleet into a decisive engagement and achieve a significant victory, influenced the German fleet's actions.

Scheer's decision to engage the British fleet aggressively and press the attack reflected his intent to break the British blockade.

Outcome and Legacy:

The Battle of Jutland ended inconclusively, with neither side achieving a decisive victory.

However, the battle had a significant impact on naval warfare, influencing tactics, ship design, and strategic thinking in subsequent naval engagements.

In conclusion, the Battle of Jutland was a complex and pivotal naval engagement, marked by several key moments and decisions that shaped its outcome and the course of naval warfare in World War I.

Actions of key commanders such as Jellicoe and Scheer

The Battle of Jutland, fought from May 31 to June 1, 1916, involved the actions of key commanders from both the British Grand Fleet and the German High Seas Fleet. Admirals John Jellicoe and Reinhard Scheer played crucial roles in shaping the strategies and decisions that influenced the outcome of the battle. Here's a look at their actions:

Admiral John Jellicoe (British Grand Fleet):

Jellicoe commanded the British Grand Fleet, the most powerful fleet in the world at the time, with the objective of engaging and defeating the German High Seas Fleet.

His cautious and strategic approach to the battle was influenced by his desire to preserve his fleet's numerical superiority and avoid unnecessary risks.

Jellicoe's decision-making during the battle focused on maintaining a defensive posture while seeking opportunities to engage the enemy fleet on favorable terms.

His leadership and tactical acumen were instrumental in preventing a decisive German victory and maintaining British control of the North Sea.

Admiral Reinhard Scheer (German High Seas Fleet):

Scheer commanded the German High Seas Fleet, which was tasked with breaking the British naval blockade and challenging British naval supremacy.

His aggressive and innovative approach to the battle was characterized by attempts to outmaneuver and outgun the British fleet.

Scheer's decision to engage the British fleet in a night action, despite the risks, demonstrated his willingness to take bold actions to achieve victory.

His tactical skills and leadership were evident in his ability to exploit weaknesses in the British fleet's formations and maneuver his fleet effectively during the battle.

Key Decisions and Actions:

Jellicoe's decision to deploy his fleet in a defensive formation and engage the German fleet at long range was a strategic choice that played to the strengths of his fleet.

Scheer's decision to turn his fleet away from the British fleet during the "Run to the South" phase of the battle was a tactical maneuver aimed at repositioning his forces for a more favorable engagement.

Both commanders made critical decisions throughout the battle that reflected their understanding of naval warfare and their determination to achieve victory for their respective fleets.

Legacy:

The actions of Jellicoe and Scheer at the Battle of Jutland had a lasting impact on naval warfare, influencing tactics, strategy, and ship design in future naval engagements.

Their leadership during the battle showcased the challenges and complexities of naval warfare in the early 20th century and highlighted the importance of decisive command decisions in battle.

In conclusion, the actions of key commanders such as Jellicoe and Scheer were instrumental in shaping the outcome of the Battle of Jutland. Their strategic and tactical decisions reflected their leadership qualities and their commitment to their respective fleets.

Tactical decisions and their impact on the outcome of the battle

The Battle of Jutland, fought on May 31 to June 1, 1916, was shaped by a series of tactical decisions made by commanders on both sides. These decisions had a significant impact on the outcome of the battle, influencing the course of naval warfare during World War I. Here are some key tactical decisions and their impact:

1.   Deployment of Battlecruisers:

The decision to deploy battlecruisers as scouting forces proved to be a critical tactical choice.

While battlecruisers were faster and had greater firepower than traditional cruisers, their thinner armor made them vulnerable to enemy fire.

This tactical decision led to the early loss of several British battlecruisers, highlighting the risks associated with their use in battle.

2.   Maneuvering and Positioning:

The maneuvering and positioning of fleets during the battle were crucial tactical decisions that determined the course of engagements.

Both sides sought to gain a favorable position relative to the enemy, using tactics such as crossing the enemy's "T" to maximize firepower while minimizing exposure.

3.   Use of Torpedo Attacks:

Both the British and German fleets employed torpedo attacks as part of their tactical arsenal.

Torpedo attacks were used to target enemy capital ships and disrupt enemy formations, with varying degrees of success.

4. Night Actions:

The decision to continue the battle into the night introduced new tactical challenges for both sides.

Reduced visibility and the difficulty of maintaining formation led to confusion and uncertainty, impacting the effectiveness of tactical decisions.

5. Command Decisions:

Commanders made critical decisions throughout the battle, including when to engage, disengage, or change course.

These decisions were influenced by factors such as intelligence, communication, and the overall strategic objectives of each fleet.

6. Impact on Outcome:

The tactical decisions made during the Battle of Jutland had a direct impact on its outcome.

The loss of key ships, the effectiveness of torpedo attacks, and the ability to maintain formation all played a role in shaping the course of the battle and its final result.

7. Legacy:

The tactical decisions made at the Battle of Jutland highlighted the evolving nature of naval warfare in the early 20th century.

Lessons learned from the battle influenced future naval tactics and strategy, shaping the development of naval warfare in the years to come.

In conclusion, the Battle of Jutland was a complex and dynamic naval engagement shaped by a series of tactical decisions. These decisions, made under the pressures of battle, had a profound impact on the outcome of the battle and the course of naval warfare during World War I.

Aftermath and Analysis

The aftermath of the Battle of Jutland, fought on May 31 to June 1, 1916, had significant implications for both the British Grand Fleet and the German High Seas Fleet. The battle, while inconclusive in terms of a clear victory for either side, had a lasting impact on naval warfare and the course of World War I. Here's an overview of the aftermath and analysis of the Battle of Jutland:

Casualties and Damage:

The Battle of Jutland resulted in heavy casualties and significant damage to both fleets.

The British lost 14 ships and over 6,000 men, while the Germans lost 11 ships and over 2,500 men.

The loss of life and ships was a major blow to both sides and highlighted the destructive power of modern naval warfare.

Strategic Impact:

Despite the heavy losses, the British Grand Fleet maintained control of the North Sea, preventing the German High Seas Fleet from achieving its objective of breaking the British blockade.

The battle did not result in a decisive victory for either side, but it did demonstrate the strength and capabilities of both fleets.

Tactical Lessons:

The Battle of Jutland led to a reassessment of naval tactics and strategies on both sides.

The vulnerabilities of battlecruisers and the importance of armor protection were key lessons learned from the battle.

Both sides also recognized the need for improved communication and coordination in future naval engagements.

Impact on Naval Warfare:

The Battle of Jutland marked the last major naval battle between battleships in history.

The increasing importance of submarines, aircraft, and aircraft carriers was highlighted, leading to a shift in focus in naval warfare.

Legacy:

The Battle of Jutland had a lasting impact on the course of World War I and naval history.

While inconclusive, the battle reinforced British naval dominance and prevented the German High Seas Fleet from posing a significant threat to British sea lanes.

The battle also shaped the development of naval technology and tactics in the years that followed, influencing future naval engagements.

In conclusion, the Battle of Jutland was a pivotal moment in naval history, with far-reaching consequences for both the British and German fleets. While it did not result in a clear victory for either side, the battle highlighted the changing nature of naval warfare and the importance of adaptability and innovation in the face of new challenges.

Assessment of the strategic outcome of the battle

The Battle of Jutland, fought on May 31 to June 1, 1916, was the largest naval battle of World War I and a crucial confrontation between the British Grand Fleet and the German High Seas Fleet. The strategic outcome of the battle was complex and subject to interpretation, as neither side achieved a decisive victory. Here's an assessment of the strategic outcome of the Battle of Jutland:

1.   British Perspective:

From the British perspective, the strategic outcome of the Battle of Jutland was generally seen as a victory.

While the British suffered greater losses in terms of ships and men, they maintained control of the North Sea and the blockade of Germany remained intact.

The British Grand Fleet, under the command of Admiral Jellicoe, demonstrated its superiority over the German High Seas Fleet and retained its strategic advantage in naval warfare.

2.   German Perspective:

From the German perspective, the strategic outcome of the Battle of Jutland was more nuanced.

While the German High Seas Fleet inflicted greater losses on the British in terms of ships sunk, they were unable to break the British blockade or achieve a decisive victory.

The German fleet, under the command of Admiral Scheer, was forced to retreat to port and did not engage in another major fleet action for the remainder of the war.

3.   Impact on Naval Strategy:

The Battle of Jutland had a significant impact on naval strategy for both sides.

The British continued to maintain a defensive posture, focusing on maintaining control of the North Sea and protecting their sea lanes.

The Germans, realizing that they could not challenge British naval supremacy directly, turned their focus to submarine warfare, leading to the unrestricted submarine warfare campaign that ultimately drew the United States into the war.

4.   Legacy:

The Battle of Jutland had a lasting impact on naval warfare, shaping the development of naval technology, tactics, and strategy in the years that followed.

The battle highlighted the importance of reconnaissance, communication, and coordination in naval engagements, as well as the need for ships with adequate armor protection.

In conclusion, the strategic outcome of the Battle of Jutland was a complex and multifaceted event that had far-reaching consequences for both British and German naval strategy. While neither side achieved a decisive victory, the battle demonstrated the changing nature of naval warfare and the challenges of modern naval combat.

Analysis of the performance of both navies and lessons learned

The Battle of Jutland, fought on May 31 to June 1, 1916, was a pivotal naval engagement between the British Grand Fleet and the German High Seas Fleet during World War I. The performance of both navies during the battle and the lessons learned from it had a significant impact on naval warfare. Here's an analysis of the performance of both navies and the lessons learned:

1.   British Performance:

The British Grand Fleet, under the command of Admiral John Jellicoe, demonstrated several strengths during the battle.

The fleet's ability to maintain formation and discipline under fire was commendable, allowing it to respond effectively to German attacks.

British gunnery was generally accurate and effective, resulting in significant damage to German ships.

However, British tactics were criticized for being overly cautious, with Jellicoe choosing to preserve his fleet rather than risk a decisive engagement.

2.   German Performance:

The German High Seas Fleet, under the command of Admiral Reinhard Scheer, also displayed strengths during the battle.

German gunnery was generally effective, with several British ships being hit and damaged.

German torpedo attacks were particularly successful, causing significant damage to British ships.

However, German tactics were criticized for being too aggressive, leading to unnecessary risks and exposing the fleet to British firepower.

3.   Lessons Learned:

The Battle of Jutland highlighted the importance of reconnaissance and intelligence in naval warfare. Both sides struggled with accurate information about the enemy's position and intentions, leading to tactical errors.

The battle underscored the vulnerability of battlecruisers to enemy fire, as demonstrated by the loss of several British and German battlecruisers.

The need for improved communication and coordination within fleets was evident, as both sides experienced difficulties in maintaining contact and control of their forces during the battle.

The importance of adaptability and flexibility in naval tactics was also emphasized, as both sides had to adjust their strategies in response to changing circumstances during the battle.

4.   Impact on Naval Warfare:

The Battle of Jutland had a profound impact on naval warfare, influencing tactics, strategy, and ship design in the years that followed.

The battle highlighted the need for improved armor protection for ships, leading to changes in the design of future warships.

It also marked the end of the era of decisive battles between battleships, as the focus of naval warfare shifted towards submarines, aircraft, and aircraft carriers.

In conclusion, the Battle of Jutland was a complex and challenging engagement that tested the capabilities of both the British and German navies. While neither side achieved a decisive victory, the battle provided valuable lessons that shaped the future of naval warfare.

Legacy and Impact

The Battle of Jutland, fought on May 31 to June 1, 1916, during World War I, left a lasting legacy and had a significant impact on naval warfare. Despite being inconclusive in terms of a clear victory for either side, the battle had several far-reaching consequences that shaped the course of naval history. Here's a look at the legacy and impact of the Battle of Jutland:

Technological Developments:

The Battle of Jutland highlighted the need for advancements in naval technology, particularly in ship design and armament.

Lessons learned from the battle led to improvements in armor protection, gunnery, and communications on future warships.

Tactical and Strategic Evolution:

The battle marked a shift in naval tactics and strategy, with an increased emphasis on fleet coordination, reconnaissance, and flexibility.

Both sides learned valuable lessons about the vulnerabilities of their fleets and the importance of adapting to changing circumstances in battle.

Impact on Naval Doctrine:

The Battle of Jutland had a profound impact on naval doctrine, influencing how navies around the world approached naval warfare.

The concept of the decisive naval battle between battleships was challenged, leading to a greater focus on naval aviation, submarines, and convoy tactics.

Psychological and Political Impact:

The inconclusive outcome of the Battle of Jutland had a significant psychological impact on both the British and German public.

In Britain, the battle was portrayed as a victory, despite the heavy losses, while in Germany, it was seen as a missed opportunity for a decisive victory.

The political ramifications of the battle were felt in both countries, with questions raised about the effectiveness of naval leadership and strategy.

Legacy of Loss:

The Battle of Jutland resulted in the loss of over 6,000 British and over 2,500 German sailors, making it one of the deadliest naval battles in history.

The legacy of those who lost their lives in the battle is remembered through memorials and commemorations in both countries.

Impact on World War I:

While the Battle of Jutland did not decisively alter the course of World War I, it did have strategic implications.

The British Grand Fleet maintained control of the North Sea, preventing the German High Seas Fleet from threatening Britain's sea lanes.

In conclusion, the Battle of Jutland left a lasting legacy and had a profound impact on naval warfare, shaping the development of naval technology, tactics, and strategy in the years that followed.

The impact of the battle on naval warfare and strategy

The Battle of Jutland, fought on May 31 to June 1, 1916, during World War I, had a significant impact on naval warfare and strategy. While the battle did not result in a decisive victory for either side, it did shape the future direction of naval tactics and operations. Here's a look at the impact of the Battle of Jutland on naval warfare and strategy:

1. End of the Era of the Decisive Battle:

The Battle of Jutland marked the end of the era of the decisive naval battle between battleships.

Both sides recognized that the risk of catastrophic losses outweighed the potential gains of a decisive engagement, leading to a more cautious approach to naval warfare.

Focus on Submarines and Unrestricted Submarine Warfare:

The inconclusive outcome of the Battle of Jutland led the Germans to focus more on submarine warfare as a means of challenging British naval supremacy.

The German use of unrestricted submarine warfare, which eventually drew the United States into World War I, was a direct result of the strategic stalemate at Jutland.

2. Development of Convoy Tactics:

The Battle of Jutland highlighted the vulnerability of ships to submarine attacks when operating independently.

This led to the development of convoy tactics, where merchant ships were grouped together and protected by naval escorts, which proved to be an effective countermeasure against submarine attacks.

3. Importance of Intelligence and Reconnaissance:

The battle underscored the importance of intelligence and reconnaissance in naval warfare.

Both sides struggled with inaccurate or incomplete information about the enemy's position and intentions, leading to tactical errors and missed opportunities.

4. Shift to Aircraft and Aircraft Carriers:

The Battle of Jutland demonstrated the potential of aircraft as reconnaissance and strike platforms in naval warfare.

This led to the development of aircraft carriers as a key component of naval fleets, as they could launch aircraft to scout enemy positions and attack enemy ships.

5. Impact on Naval Technology:

The battle highlighted the need for improvements in naval technology, particularly in ship design, armor protection, and gunnery.

Lessons learned from the battle influenced the development of future warships and naval weaponry.

6. Legacy of Caution:

The inconclusive outcome of the Battle of Jutland and the heavy losses suffered by both sides left a legacy of caution in naval warfare.

Naval commanders became more risk-averse, preferring to avoid large-scale fleet engagements unless the odds were heavily in their favor.

In conclusion, the Battle of Jutland had a profound impact on naval warfare and strategy, shaping the development of naval tactics, technology, and doctrine in the years that followed. It marked the beginning of a new era in naval warfare, characterized by a shift away from the decisive battles of the past towards more cautious and nuanced approaches to naval operations.

Commemoration and remembrance of the battle's participants

The Battle of Jutland, fought on May 31 to June 1, 1916, during World War I, left a lasting impact on the participants and their families. The commemoration and remembrance of those who fought in the battle have been an important aspect of naval history and military tradition. Here's a look at how the battle's participants have been commemorated and remembered:

1.   Memorials and Monuments:

Numerous memorials and monuments have been erected to honor the participants of the Battle of Jutland.

In the United Kingdom, the Portsmouth Naval Memorial and the Chatham Naval Memorial are dedicated to the sailors who lost their lives in the battle.

In Germany, the Laboe Naval Memorial near Kiel commemorates the sailors of the German High Seas Fleet who died in the battle.

2.   Remembrance Services:

Remembrance services are held annually to honor the participants of the Battle of Jutland.

These services often include wreath-laying ceremonies, readings of names, and moments of silence to remember those who lost their lives.

3.   Personal Stories and Accounts:

The personal stories and accounts of those who fought in the Battle of Jutland have been preserved and shared to ensure that their experiences are not forgotten.

These accounts provide valuable insights into the challenges and sacrifices faced by the participants of the battle.

4.   Educational Programs:

Educational programs and initiatives have been developed to educate the public about the Battle of Jutland and its significance.

These programs often include exhibitions, lectures, and publications to ensure that the memory of the battle is preserved for future generations.

5. Military Tradition:

The Battle of Jutland is commemorated as a key event in naval history and is often cited as an example of the bravery and sacrifice of those who serve in the navy.

The battle's participants are remembered as heroes who fought bravely in defense of their countries and their ideals.

In conclusion, the Battle of Jutland and its participants are commemorated and remembered in various ways to ensure that their sacrifice and courage are never forgotten. Through memorials, remembrance services, personal accounts, and educational programs, the memory of the Battle of Jutland lives on, reminding us of the human cost of war and the importance of honoring those who have served.

Historiography and Controversies

The Battle of Jutland, fought on May 31 to June 1, 1916, during World War I, has been the subject of extensive historiography and has generated various controversies over the years. Historiography refers to the study of how historical events have been interpreted and understood by different historians over time. Here's an overview of the historiography and controversies surrounding the Battle of Jutland:

Initial Interpretations:

In the immediate aftermath of the battle, both the British and German governments released official accounts that sought to portray the battle in a favorable light for their respective navies.

These accounts often downplayed losses and highlighted successes to boost morale and maintain public support for the war effort.

Post-War Analysis:

In the years following World War I, a more critical examination of the Battle of Jutland began to emerge.

Historians and naval experts analyzed the tactics, decisions, and outcomes of the battle, leading to a more nuanced understanding of its significance.

Revisionist Interpretations:

In the latter half of the 20th century, revisionist historians began to challenge some of the established narratives surrounding the Battle of Jutland.

These historians questioned the effectiveness of British naval leadership and strategy, as well as the impact of the battle on the course of the war.

Controversies:

One of the key controversies surrounding the Battle of Jutland is the question of whether it was a strategic victory for either side.

Some historians argue that the battle was inconclusive and did not significantly alter the course of the war, while others contend that it was a strategic victory for the British, as it preserved their naval dominance.

Legacy and Impact:

The historiography of the Battle of Jutland continues to evolve as new evidence and perspectives emerge.

The battle's legacy and impact on naval warfare and strategy remain subjects of debate among historians and naval experts.

In conclusion, the Battle of Jutland has been the subject of extensive historiography and has generated various controversies over the years. While the battle's outcome and significance continue to be debated, its place in naval history as one of the largest and most significant naval battles of World War I is undisputed.

Different historical interpretations of the battle

The Battle of Jutland, fought on May 31 to June 1, 1916, during World War I, has been subject to various historical interpretations over the years. Different historians and scholars have analyzed the battle from different perspectives, leading to a range of interpretations regarding its significance and outcome. Here are some of the key historical interpretations of the Battle of Jutland:

1.   Strategic Victory vs. Tactical Stalemate:

One of the main points of contention among historians is whether the Battle of Jutland was a strategic victory for either side or merely a tactical stalemate.

Some argue that the British Grand Fleet, despite suffering heavier losses, achieved its strategic objective of maintaining control of the North Sea, thus securing a strategic victory.

Others contend that the battle did not decisively alter the balance of power in the North Sea and therefore should be considered a tactical stalemate.

2.   Impact on the War:

Historians also differ in their views on the impact of the Battle of Jutland on the course of World War I.

Some argue that the battle marked a turning point in the war, as it prevented the German High Seas Fleet from posing a significant threat to Britain's sea lanes and thus contributed to the eventual Allied victory.

Others maintain that the battle did not have a decisive impact on the outcome of the war and that other factors, such as the entry of the United States into the conflict, were more decisive.

3. Assessment of Leadership:

The performance of naval commanders, particularly Admiral John Jellicoe of the British Grand Fleet and Admiral Reinhard Scheer of the German High Seas Fleet, has been a subject of debate among historians.

Some historians criticize Jellicoe for his cautious approach to the battle, arguing that he missed opportunities to achieve a more decisive victory.

Others defend Jellicoe's decisions, noting the challenges he faced in maintaining control of his fleet and avoiding a catastrophic defeat.

4. Technological and Tactical Lessons:

Historians have also analyzed the technological and tactical lessons learned from the Battle of Jutland.

The battle highlighted the importance of armor protection, ship design, and gunnery accuracy in naval warfare, leading to advancements in these areas in the years that followed.

The use of submarines, aircraft, and convoy tactics also emerged as important lessons from the battle.

In conclusion, the Battle of Jutland remains a subject of historical debate, with different interpretations regarding its significance, outcome, and impact on naval warfare. The diverse range of historical perspectives on the battle reflects its complexity and the challenges inherent in interpreting historical events.

Controversies surrounding key aspects of the battle and its aftermath

The Battle of Jutland, fought on May 31 to June 1, 1916, during World War I, has been the subject of numerous controversies surrounding key aspects of the battle and its aftermath. These controversies have arisen from differing interpretations of the events of the battle, as well as the decisions made by naval commanders and governments. Here are some of the key controversies surrounding the Battle of Jutland:

1.   Strategic Outcome:

One of the main controversies surrounding the Battle of Jutland is the question of whether it was a strategic victory for either side.

Some historians argue that the British Grand Fleet, despite suffering heavier losses, achieved its strategic objective of maintaining control of the North Sea, thus securing a strategic victory.

Others contend that the battle did not decisively alter the balance of power in the North Sea and therefore should be considered a tactical stalemate.

2.   Command Decisions:

The decisions made by Admiral John Jellicoe of the British Grand Fleet and Admiral Reinhard Scheer of the German High Seas Fleet during the battle have been the subject of controversy.

Some historians criticize Jellicoe for his cautious approach to the battle, arguing that he missed opportunities to achieve a more decisive victory.

Others defend Jellicoe's decisions, noting the challenges he faced in maintaining control of his fleet and avoiding a catastrophic defeat.

3.   Losses and Casualties:

The extent of losses and casualties suffered by both sides during the Battle of Jutland has been a point of controversy.

Estimates of the number of ships sunk and sailors killed vary, with some sources providing higher or lower figures than others.

The controversy over losses and casualties has led to debates about the conduct of the battle and the effectiveness of naval tactics.

4.   Intelligence and Reconnaissance:

The effectiveness of intelligence and reconnaissance efforts leading up to the Battle of Jutland has also been a subject of controversy.

Some historians argue that both sides failed to gather accurate and timely intelligence about the enemy's position and intentions, leading to tactical errors and missed opportunities.

Others contend that the challenges of gathering intelligence in a wartime environment were significant and that both sides did the best they could with the information available.

5.   Impact on the War:

The impact of the Battle of Jutland on the course of World War I has been a topic of debate among historians.

Some argue that the battle marked a turning point in the war, as it prevented the German High Seas Fleet from posing a significant threat to Britain's sea lanes.

Others maintain that the battle did not have a decisive impact on the outcome of the war and that other factors, such as the entry of the United States into the conflict, were more decisive.

In conclusion, the Battle of Jutland continues to be a subject of controversy and debate among historians and naval experts. The differing interpretations of the events of the battle and its aftermath reflect the complexity of naval warfare and the challenges of interpreting historical events.

Milton Keynes UK
Ingram Content Group UK Ltd.
UKHW010635240424
441619UK00001BA/68

9 788119 438235